FEVER-TREE
EASY MIXING

FEVER-TREE
EASY MIXING

**MORE THAN
150 QUICK AND
DELICIOUS MIXED
DRINKS AND COCKTAILS**

MITCHELL BEAZLEY

First published in Great Britain in 2021 by Mitchell Beazley, an imprint of
Octopus Publishing Group Ltd
Carmelite House
50 Victoria Embankment
London EC4Y 0DZ
www.octopusbooks.co.uk

An Hachette UK Company
www.hachette.co.uk

Distributed in the US by Hachette Book Group
1290 Avenue of the Americas
4th and 5th Floors
New York, NY 10104

Distributed in Canada by Canadian Manda Group
664 Annette Street
Toronto, Ontario, Canada M6S 2C8

ISBN 978-1-78472-783-3

A CIP catalogue record for this book is available from the British Library.

Printed and bound in China.

10 9 8 7 6 5 4 3 2 1

All recipes serve one unless otherwise stated.

Fever-Tree Contributors: Tim Warrillow, Craig Harper, Oliver Winters,
Florence Wong, Jaz Arwand, Gavin Bruce and David Barber
Consultant Writers: Joseph Bullmore and Jonathan Wells

Group Publishing Director: Denise Bates
Senior Editor: Pauline Bache
Art Director: Yasia Williams-Leedham
Copyeditor: Sarah Reece
Photographer: Issy Croker
Mixologist: Missy Flynn
Stylist: Emily Ezekiel
Illustrator: Tamara Vodden
Senior Production Manager: Katherine Hockley

Pictured recipes are denoted with »

CONTENTS

INTRODUCTION

Fever-Tree began in 2003 with a meeting of minds and one simple premise: if ¾s of your G&T is the tonic, wouldn't you want it to be the very best?

Since our co-founders Charles and Tim put the lid on the first bottle of our Premium Indian Tonic Water, we haven't wavered in that single-minded mission, with the team travelling the globe to find the highest-quality ingredients. Whether it's Tim heading to the Democratic Republic of Congo to source our quinine or to the Yucatán Peninsula in Mexico to meet our citrus growers, or Charles travelling to the Ivory Coast and India to learn about different varieties of ginger or, closer to home, our Head of Innovation Rose making the slightly shorter journey to the fields of Norfolk to find our rhubarb, we've always aimed to bring quality, flavour and choice to you through the best ingredients that nature has to offer. And in doing so, the Fever-Tree family has grown from our solitary Premium Indian Tonic Water (of which we are still very proud, as you often are with your firstborn!) to include a range of mixers – from flavoured tonics, ginger ales and sodas, to lemonades and cola – to pair perfectly with the growing numbers of great-tasting spirits that are being created around the world.

'To pair perfectly' – sometimes it's easier said than done. Being in a cocktail bar is an incredible experience, complete with dexterous flicks, flaming fruits, elaborate twists and glittering utensils. But at home there are plenty of opportunites to enjoy amazing, easy and refreshing drinks.

So we're letting you in on a little secret. Wonderful-tasting drinks don't have to be complicated or time-consuming! And you certainly don't need arcane instruments or obscure ingredients to make them. (Feel free, however, to chuck in as many elaborate twirls as you see fit.) We have created this whole book on that very premise. Here you'll find a set of simple recipes, delicious drink ideas and straightforward instructions to help you get on with what really matters – enjoying the drink in your glass.

Happy mixing!

TECHNIQUES

Drinking well isn't difficult. If you start with a great recipe, good-quality ingredients and a few simple techniques, you'll find the drinking part takes care of itself. With that in mind, we've outlined a few tricks of the trade below, to help you get the most out of this book. (It's worth noting that things can get a little more complicated and time-consuming once you start to make several drinks at once, which is why we've included a section in the book on multiple serves and pitchers too, so that your guests don't need to go thirsty for long.)

Measuring

In cocktail making, as in cooking, proportion is more important than precise measurements being met (we've even used an egg cup to measure out drinks before). The standard spirits measure in the UK is 25ml (5 teaspoons) – 30ml is closer to 1fl oz, or 2 tablespoons. Here are some handy conversions:

    10ml = 2 teaspoons
    15ml = 3 teaspoons
    20ml = 4 teaspoons
    25ml = 5 teaspoons
    30ml = 2 tablespoons
    35ml = 2 generous tablespoons
    50ml = 2fl oz

If you keep the proportions consistent, and don't mix your measures, however, the drink will remain balanced.

Building a drink

Every recipe in the book can be 'built'. This is the simplest way to create a cocktail and doesn't require anything more than ingredients, ice and a glass. Here's an example of a built recipe:

Pour 50ml (2fl oz) of Plymouth Gin into an ice-filled copa or large wine glass. Top up with Fever-Tree Premium Indian Tonic Water. Garnish with an orange wedge and a lemon wedge.

Sounds simple doesn't it? And that's the point: it is simple. To follow this recipe, all you need to do is first select a suitable glass – in this instance a copa or large wine glass (see page 16) – place it on a flat, stable surface and fill it at least three-quarters full with ice cubes. You would then measure out 50ml (2fl oz) of Plymouth Gin and pour it into the glass over the ice. Open your tonic water and fill to a finger's width below the rim (approximately 200ml/7fl oz – or a little more or less, depending on taste or strength preferred), before cutting a wedge of orange and a wedge of lemon and adding them to the glass.

Ice

Ice is almost as important an ingredient as the gin and the tonic. You will need lots of it. Each ice cube is like a little battery of coldness – if you only put two or three into a lovely big G&T, they'll have to work extra hard to chill the drink. And when ice works hard, it uses more energy, and turns more quickly back into water. If you put lots of ice into a drink, however, all those cubes work together to get the liquid to an ideal temperature quickly, and then maintain it. Essentially, more ice cubes in your glass means a colder drink that stays stronger for longer. So, fill your glass three-quarters full with ice cubes to begin with, and you'll be on the right track.

One last tip: when having friends round for drinks, always buy or make twice as much ice as you think you'll need. In our experience, that's usually the right amount. (If you only have one ice-cube tray, make extra in advance and store it in a clean, empty ice-cream tub.)

Shaking

Some of the 'With a Twist' versions of the recipes in this book require you to shake your cocktail while making it. We shake a drink when we really need to mix up the ingredients. This is important for soft fruits or herbs, like raspberries or mint, as it breaks them up and disperses the flavour evenly throughout the drink. It's also beneficial when working with a thicker substance, such as a jam or syrup or a purée, for the same reason.

You can shake a drink in anything that's watertight and that won't break due to impact or the temperature of the cocktail. A cocktail shaker is ideal, but a blender cup with screw-top lid or a large plastic water bottle will do the job too – as long as there's room for all the ingredients and a decent scoop of ice cubes, and enough free space left for the drink to circulate when you shake it. And you really do need to shake it – like dancing, you should shake like no-one's watching – since at least 15 seconds of vigorous jostling is necessary to get the job done. During the shaking, the ingredients and ice cubes will begin to break up. At this point, in a bar setting, the liquid would be strained out into a glass filled with fresh ice cubes. For at-home mixing, however, it works just as well simply to open up the shaker and pour all the contents into a glass, perhaps topping up with a little fresh ice before you add your tonic water or mixer.

An important note – don't shake your Fever-Tree mixers. You don't want to waste all the beautiful bubbles, so these should always be added after the other ingredients have been shaken.

Cutting fruit

To get the most out of your citrus fruit, it's always best to cut it around its middle, along the 'equator' line, as opposed to top to bottom. A horizontal cut pierces all the individual fleshy cells of the fruit and allows you uninhibited access to the wonderful juice inside. You can expect to get approximately six wedges from a whole lemon or lime, and ten from a good-sized orange.

In some of the recipes, you'll need to squeeze over the juice from the citrus wedge first, and then drop it in. This allows the tart flavours to escape immediately, rather than releasing slowly, and also gets some of the oils from the skin into the mix.

Creating a twist of peel

Some recipes suggest adding a twist of citrus peel as a garnish. This technique is all about accessing the aromatic oils only in the skin of the fruit. You need to cut the colourful skin away from the white pith below, and then bend or twist the skin over the drink. Probably the easiest way to accomplish this is with a vegetable peeler (also great to make longer, ribbon-like garnishes of citrus or cucumber). A peeler sprays the oils while it trims the skin – so be sure to hold the fruit over the top of the glass while you're working on it and the oils will add the most wonderful aroma to your drink. Place the citrus peel with the outside facing the drink so that the oils infuse into the drink.

Slapping herbs

This technique releases the maximum flavour from a herb garnish so that when your nose approaches the glass, it is immediately met by heady scents and perfumed notes. Place the mint (or thyme, rosemary or other aromatic herb) in one hand and clap down hard and swiftly with the other. This will break some of the plant's cell walls and unlock the oils that hold all those potent aromas. Finally, place the herb at the side of the drink that you intend to sip from, to better direct the fragrance towards your nose as you drink.

Stirring and muddling

The carbonation in our mixers will do a great job of blending all the liquid components of your drink together. When adding something like a jam or a syrup, however, or if using mint or a soft fruit, it can be helpful to give the liquid a stir too. Using a long spoon, pull up from the bottom of the glass to get an even spread throughout the drink. When using fruits, it can also be useful to muddle – which means to crush the fruit on to the bottom of the glass before adding the other ingredients. You can use a wooden spoon or a pestle. (It's often easier, however, to shake drinks instead of muddling, plus it gives a more consistent result.)

Sugar syrup, agave syrup and honey

Sugar syrup is available from most large supermarkets and shop-bought versions tend to last longer and dissolve more easily than homemade options. But it's simple to make at home, with a 2:1 ratio of caster sugar and boiling water, stirred until completely dissolved. (If you have a sweet tooth or prefer things less sweet, then feel free to play around and adjust the proportions to taste.) You can make extra and store it in a sterilized (run through a hot cycle in the dishwasher to sterilize), sealed bottle.

Agave syrup is a sweetener made from the agave plant, which tequila also comes from — meaning the pair work together particularly well.

Honey is best diluted with warm water in a 1:1 ratio when used in drinks, to ensure it dissolves properly. If adding raw honey directly to a drink, add to the spirit first and stir until it dissolves, before adding ice cubes.

While we have specified which sweetener to use in each cocktail, you can always substitute one for another when supplies are running low.

EQUIPMENT

A good, sharp knife: essential for cutting fruit.

A vegetable peeler: great for cutting twists of citrus peel or making longer ribbon garnishes with cucumber, etc.

A cocktail shaker: useful, but a blender cup with a screw-top lid, a Mason jar or a large water bottle will work too (see page 11). As long as what you use is large enough to contain the liquid for one drink and ice, and has room to spare when you shake it, it'll do a fine job. If it's big enough for two drinks, even better.

GLASSES

Great-tasting drinks don't have to be presented in fancy glasses. Here are a few glasses that we like and that complement our drinks well:

 Copa/large wine glass: Your glass should be able to hold at least 400ml (14fl oz) – up to 500ml (17fl oz) is even better, as it allows room for more ice cubes and garnishes.

 Highball/Collins: A tall glass that should be able to hold 400–500ml (14–17fl oz). Excellent for long drinks.

 Rocks/tumbler: Most of our drinks have been put together with the slightly larger highball or wine glass in mind, but these glasses can be good when sharing a pitcher.

We've suggested a particular glass for each recipe in the book, best suited to that particular cocktail, but don't worry if you haven't got the exact one. Our drinks will taste good drunk out of any glass!

G&T
& FRIENDS

1

G&T & FRIENDS

These days, at certain times of the year and in certain greetings card shops, you may begin to notice a nifty little refrain dotted about the place: 'You are the gin to my tonic'. You will spot it on Valentine's Day cards and wall plaques; on bumper stickers and key rings, and chalk boards. It comes in red and pink hues, and in flowing script fonts accompanied by hearts. And you don't need to be a mixologist or a professional matchmaker to divine the meaning. To be compared to one half of this humble mix — this happy union — is the highest praise we might give our nearest and dearest. You know a drink has made it when it's begun to replace 'I love you' in the romance stakes.

Not that this trend is all that surprising. Because the partnership of gin and tonic is a love affair of quite poetic proportions. Theirs is the greatest marriage of all — and it started in sickness as much as in health. Gin, a spirit distilled with juniper, dates back at least 900 years, when it was usually taken as a medicine against ailments and disease. The earliest traces of the drink exist in Salerno, Italy, where Benedictine monks (it's often the monks, you'll find) translated Chinese and Arabic recipes to distill *aqua vitae* — the water of life. Soon, the Italians added flavour, as Italians tend to, via roots and herbs and spices, before the congenial influence of the Dutch saw this 'genever' sashay out from the medicine cabinet forever — and over to the bar. Before you knew it, the English were in on the act too, with the creation of their epoch-defining London Dry: the style of gin most recognized and sipped today.

But it wasn't until the 18th century that the spirit finally met its soulmate. By then, the European armies had discovered that malaria, rampant in the tropics, was striking down their men at an alarming rate. They turned to the ancient wisdom of the Americas, and the healing bark of the cinchona tree (also known as the fever tree) — a rare and delicate plant that thrived in the foothills of the High Andes and produced quinine, a preventative for the deadly disease. By 1865, the Briton Charles Ledger had smuggled cinchona seeds out of the Peruvian rainforest, and Europeans had succeeded in growing the medicinal tree themselves.

The only problem was that quinine itself is incredibly bitter. In fact, the only way to get soldiers to drink it was to mix it with water, citrus and sugar. Adding their daily ration of gin didn't hurt either, of course — and for many, it was love at first sip. Or as Winston Churchill wrote: 'Gin and tonic has saved more Englishmen's lives, and minds, than all the doctors in the Empire.'

When we began making tonic at Fever-Tree, we wanted to restore this fantastic ingredient to its rightful place in our recipe. That's why we spent our first 18 months delving into the history books discovering its origins and then set out to track down the finest possible cinchona trees in the world — taking us to a set of plantations spread like vineyards across the eastern Democratic Republic of Congo that were descended from the very same seeds Charles Ledger took from Peru centuries ago.

Today, of course, the disease-proofing necessity of tonic has largely faded. But the love affair of gin and tonic has not. You don't need a greetings card company to remind you that this humble drink is the pinnacle of romance and camaraderie — an exquisite combination, the perfect match, the ultimate coalition. You just need to sip what's in your glass.

PAIRINGS

At Fever-Tree, we often get asked 'Which gin should I pair with this tonic?' or 'Which tonic should I pair with this gin?' or even 'What mixer would work best with this vodka?' Our pairing wheel has helped many people to answer these questions over the years, but it's worth explaining how the wheel came about.

When we first made our Premium Indian Tonic Water in 2004, the gin world was mostly still the domain of classic London Dry gins like Tanqueray and Beefeater, and our tonic was made to be a perfect match for these juniper-forward beauties. At the same time, our co-founders, Tim and Charles, recognized that with the wealth of modern and flavoured gins beginning to appear across the globe, we would need to keep searching for new ingredients to pair perfectly in this brave new world. This is why our innovation and ingredient hunting are so important to us, and have led to our creating a wide range of tonics to complement the now wonderfully diverse gin category.

Here, we have divided the Fever-Tree range into flavour profiles for you to find the perfect match for whichever gin you are drinking. We have included some of our favourite gins around the wheel to help you, but it's not an exhaustive list by any means. If your gin is not listed here, you'll find tasting notes for it on the bottle to see where it falls on the wheel. Or, even better, open it and decide for yourself!

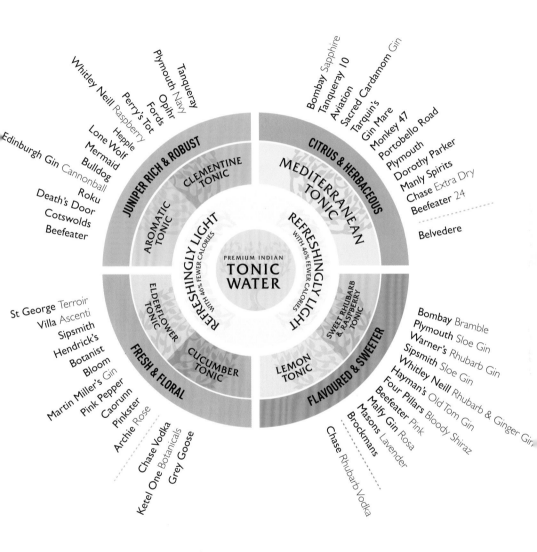

JUNIPER RICH & ROBUST

CITRUS & HERBACEOUS

FRESH & FLORAL

FLAVOURED & SWEETER

CLEMENTINE TONIC

AROMATIC TONIC

ELDERFLOWER TONIC

CUCUMBER TONIC

LEMON TONIC

SWEET RHUBARB & RASPBERRY TONIC

MEDITERRANEAN TONIC

REFRESHINGLY LIGHT WITH 46% FEWER CALORIES

REFRESHINGLY LIGHT WITH 46% FEWER CALORIES

PREMIUM INDIAN
TONIC WATER

Tanqueray
Plymouth Navy
Opihr
Fords
Perry's Tot
Whitley Neill Raspberry
Hepple
Lone Wolf
Mermaid
Bulldog
Edinburgh Gin Cannonball
Roku
Death's Door
Cotswolds
Beefeater

Bombay Sapphire
Tanqueray 10
Aviation
Sacred Cardamom Gin
Tarquin's
Gin Mare
Monkey 47
Portobello Road
Plymouth
Dorothy Parker
Manly Spirits
Chase Extra Dry
Beefeater 24

Belvedere

St George Terroir
Villa Ascenti
Sipsmith
Hendrick's
Botanist
Bloom
Martin Miller's Gin
Pink Pepper
Caorunn
Pinkster
Archie Rose

Chase Vodka
Ketel One Botanicals
Grey Goose

Bombay Bramble
Plymouth Sloe Gin
Warner's Rhubarb Gin
Sipsmith Sloe Gin
Whitley Neill Rhubarb & Ginger Gin
Hayman's Old Tom Gin
Four Pillars Bloody Shiraz
Beefeater Pink
Malfy Gin Rosa
Masons Lavender
Brockmans

Chase Rhubarb Vodka

Aside from the world of gin, vodkas are famously versatile, so we have also included some perfect pairings for a classic vodka and tonic combination. Premium vodkas allow their ingredients to shine through – take the peppery rye of Belvedere, amplified by the hints of lemon thyme in our Mediterranean Tonic Water, or the sweet winter wheat of Grey Goose, offset perfectly by the refreshing notes of our Cucumber Tonic Water or our floral Elderflower Tonic Water.

CLASSIC G&T

A simple yet elegant drink to start. The bold orange, earthy juniper and rich botanicals of Plymouth Gin work wonderfully well with our Premium Indian Tonic Water, swirling together to create a sumptuous spin on a classic G&T. It's full-bodied, fine-bubbled and looks fantastic garnished with lemon and orange.

»

- 50ml (2fl oz) Plymouth Gin
- Fever-Tree Premium Indian Tonic Water, to top up
- Orange wedge, to garnish
- Lemon wedge, to garnish

Pour the gin into a copa or large wine glass over ice cubes and top up with the tonic water. Garnish with an orange and a lemon wedge.

WITH A TWIST

- 2 orange wedges, plus an extra wedge to garnish
- 1 lemon wedge, plus an extra wedge to garnish
- 50ml (2fl oz) Plymouth Gin
- 2 teaspoons vanilla sugar, or sugar syrup (see page 15)
- Fever-Tree Premium Indian Tonic Water, to top up

Squeeze the orange wedges and the lemon wedge and drop them into an empty cocktail shaker. Add the gin and the vanilla sugar or sugar syrup, and plenty of ice cubes. Shake vigorously for 15 seconds. Pour the contents of the shaker into a copa glass and top up with the tonic water. Garnish with the extra orange and lemon wedges.

ORANGE & ROSEMARY

In Spain, herby rosemary and big juicy oranges can be found growing together on the sun-soaked southern coast. They also make a sparkling combination in the glass, so we've combined the two here and added Tanqueray No. Ten, a gin famously distilled alongside whole limes and grapefruits.

«

- 35ml (2 generous tablespoons) Tanqueray No. Ten Gin
- 3 teaspoons Cointreau or Grand Marnier
- Fever-Tree Mediterranean Tonic Water, to top up
- Long twist of orange peel, to garnish
- Small rosemary sprig, to garnish

Pour the gin into a copa or wine glass over ice cubes. Add the Cointreau or Grand Marnier and top up with the tonic water. Squeeze over the twist of orange peel to release the oils, then drop it into the glass to garnish. Add a small rosemary sprig on top.

WITH A TWIST

- 35ml (2 generous tablespoons) Tanqueray No. Ten Gin
- 3 teaspoons Cointreau or Grand Marnier
- ¼ orange
- Small rosemary sprig
- Fever-Tree Mediterranean Tonic Water, to top up

Pour the gin into an empty cocktail shaker. Add the Cointreau or Grand Marnier and squeeze in the juice from the orange quarter. Add the small rosemary sprig and plenty of ice cubes. Shake vigorously for 15 seconds. Remove the rosemary sprig and pour both the liquid and the ice into a wine glass. Top up with the tonic water.

>>> When adding herbs to drinks, bear in mind how pungent they are. You can get away with a lot of mint, but rosemary should be used sparingly.

MEDITERRANEAN G&T

This drink is brimming with the wonderful, natural flavours of the Mediterranean. Gin Mare is distilled with local olives in a 13th-century chapel just outside Barcelona. It mixes beautifully with Fever-Tree Mediterranean Tonic Water, which is made using thyme grown by the third generation of the Vidal family in Provence.

- 50ml (2fl oz) Gin Mare
- Fever-Tree Mediterranean Tonic Water, to top up
- Olive, to garnish
- Thyme sprig, to garnish

Pour the Gin Mare into a copa or large wine glass filled with ice cubes. Top up with the tonic water. Garnish with an olive and a thyme sprig.

WITH A TWIST »

- 35ml (2 generous tablespoons) Gin Mare
- 3 teaspoons dry vermouth, such as Noilly Prat Original Dry
- 1 lemon wedge
- Fever-Tree Mediterranean Tonic Water, to top up
- Olive, to garnish
- Thyme sprig, to garnish

Pour the Gin Mare into a copa or wine glass filled with ice cubes. Add the vermouth. Squeeze over and then drop in the lemon wedge. Top up with the tonic water. Garnish with an olive and a thyme sprig.

>>> Rosé vermouth or sweet vermouth will also work well here if you don't have any dry vermouth.

MINT & THYME VODKA & TONIC

We bring mint and thyme together in the kitchen, so why not combine them for a cocktail? A couple of sprigs will bring out the zing and zest of Ketel One's Citroen Vodka in this simple, summery drink. Remember to give those mint leaves a good slap, or tear them gently, to tease out the herb's fresh, fragrant flavours.

- 50ml (2fl oz) Ketel One Citroen Vodka
- 1 lemon wedge
- Fever-Tree Mediterranean Tonic Water, to top up
- A handful of mint leaves, plus an extra sprig to garnish
- Thyme sprig, to garnish

Pour the vodka into a copa or large wine glass filled with ice cubes. Squeeze over and then drop in the lemon wedge. Top up with the tonic water. Slap the mint leaves to release their aromas (see page 12), then add them to the glass. Garnish with a mint sprig and a thyme sprig.

« WITH A TWIST

- Small bunch of mint leaves, plus an extra sprig to garnish
- 2 thyme sprigs, plus an extra sprig to garnish
- 3 lemon wedges
- 50ml (2fl oz) Ketel One Citroen Vodka
- 2 teaspoons sugar syrup (see page 15)
- Fever-Tree Mediterranean Tonic Water, to top up

Put the mint leaves and thyme sprigs into an empty cocktail shaker. Squeeze over and then drop in the lemon wedges. Pour over the vodka and the sugar syrup. Add plenty of ice cubes and shake vigorously for 15 seconds, then pour the contents of the shaker into a copa or wine glass. Top up with the tonic water and garnish with a mint sprig and a thyme sprig.

ENGLISH GARDEN

In this thirst-quenching drink, the lush, floral flavour of
elderflower sits beautifully alongside sharp, refreshing mint.
Add lemon into the summery mix, and you've got a crisp, cooling
cocktail that takes just seconds to throw together.

«

- 50ml (2fl oz) Tanqueray No. Ten Gin
- Fever-Tree Elderflower Tonic Water, to top up
- Mint sprig, to garnish

Pour the gin into a copa or wine glass filled with ice cubes.
Top up with the tonic water. Garnish with a mint sprig.

WITH A TWIST

- 50ml (2fl oz) Tanqueray No. Ten Gin
- 2 lemon wedges
- 2 teaspoons sugar syrup (see page 15)
- Fever-Tree Elderflower Tonic Water, to top up
- Mint sprig, to garnish

Pour the gin into an empty cocktail shaker. Add the lemon wedges and the sugar
syrup. Add plenty of ice cubes. Shake vigorously for 15 seconds, then pour the
contents of the shaker into a copa or wine glass. Top up with the tonic water and
garnish with a mint sprig.

> > >   To release the full aroma from mint leaves, 'wake them up' by clapping them between your
hands, to bruise the leaves (see page 12).

ELDERFLOWER & RASPBERRY

When you add the sweet punch of raspberry to delicate elderflower, the two flavours blossom into something completely new. The combination of fruity Chambord liqueur, floral elderflower and sharp lemon creates a deep, rich drink with a lightly refreshing edge.

»

- 35ml (2 generous tablespoons) premium vodka or gin (we like Bombay Sapphire if using gin)
- 3 teaspoons Chambord
- 1 lemon wedge
- Fever-Tree Elderflower Tonic Water, to top up
- Raspberry, to garnish

Pour the gin and Chambord into a highball glass filled with ice cubes. Squeeze over and add in the lemon wedge. Top up with the tonic water and garnish with a fresh raspberry.

WITH A TWIST

- 35ml (2 generous tablespoons) premium vodka or gin
- 3 teaspoons Chambord
- 1 lemon wedge
- A handful of raspberries
- Fever-Tree Elderflower Tonic Water, to top up

Add all the ingredients except the tonic water to an empty cocktail shaker. Add plenty of ice cubes. Shake vigorously for 15 seconds, then pour the contents of the shaker into a copa or wine glass. Top up with the tonic water.

>>> If you don't have any Chambord, you can add 1 teaspoon of raspberry jam instead to replicate the flavour. Ensure you stir the drink gently but thoroughly so that the jam dissolves. If you do this, make sure you change your vodka or gin measure to 50ml (2fl oz).

CHERRY BLOSSOM

This may be the perfect pink G&T, but it starts off with oranges.
Tanqueray Flor de Sevilla Gin gives the drink a fruity citrus base,
which blends wonderfully with the gentle sweetness of the kirsch.
With the tonic's aromatic botanicals of angostura bark, cardamom
and pimento berry, this makes the tastiest, pinkest drink around.

- 50ml (2fl oz) Tanqueray Flor de Sevilla Gin
- 1 cherry from a jar, plus 1 teaspoon kirsch from the jar
- Fever-Tree Aromatic Tonic Water, to top up
- Orange wedge, to garnish

Pour the gin into a wine glass filled with ice cubes. Add the cherry and
kirsch from the jar. Top up with the tonic water
and garnish with an orange wedge.

WITH A TWIST »

- 35ml (2 generous tablespoons) Tanqueray Flor de Sevilla Gin
- 35ml (2 generous tablespoons) dry white vermouth
- 1 cherry from a jar, plus 1 teaspoon kirsch from the jar
- 1 lemon, halved
- 1 orange, halved, plus an extra wedge to garnish
- Fever-Tree Aromatic Tonic Water, to top up

Fill a wine glass with ice cubes. Pour in the gin and vermouth. Add the cherry and kirsch from the
jar. Squeeze over the lemon and the orange halves and then drop them in. Top up with the tonic
water. Garnish with an orange wedge.

>>> You can use cherries in syrup here, but cherries in kirsch or brandy will have more flavour, as
will the liquid in the jar!

AROMATIC ORANGE

This juicy orange twist on a classic G&T is incredibly refreshing. Seville oranges have been used as a botanical in Beefeater Gin for over one hundred years, and the addition of both Fever-Tree Aromatic Tonic Water and orange liqueur really teases out that sweet-tart flavour. All that's left is to garnish with a generous orange wedge.

«

- 50ml (2fl oz) Beefeater Gin
- Fever-Tree Aromatic Tonic Water, to top up
- Orange wedge, to garnish

Pour the gin into a highball glass filled with ice cubes. Top up with the tonic water and garnish with an orange wedge.

WITH A TWIST

- 35ml (2 generous tablespoons) Beefeater Gin
- 3 teaspoons Cointreau or Grand Marnier
- Fever-Tree Aromatic Tonic Water, to top up
- Orange wedge, to garnish
- Small rosemary sprig, to garnish

Fill a highball glass with ice cubes. Add the gin and the Cointreau or Grand Marnier. Top up with the tonic water. Garnish with an orange wedge and a small rosemary sprig.

>>> If you don't have any orange liqueur, you could squeeze orange wedges over the glass and drop in instead. If you do this, make sure you increase your gin measure to 50ml (2fl oz).

CUCUMBER & MINT

Mint and cucumber are a match made in heaven. The herby sweetness of the mint marries perfectly with the mild, refreshing cucumber. With Sipsmith London Dry Gin, boasting botanicals of Seville orange peel and Spanish lemon zest, poured over, this fresh take on a classic G&T is as cool as, well…a cucumber!

- 50ml (2fl oz) Sipsmith London Dry Gin
- Fever-Tree Cucumber Tonic Water, to top up
- 3 thin cucumber slices, to garnish
- Mint sprig, to garnish

Add the gin to a copa or wine glass filled with ice cubes. Top up with the tonic water. Garnish with the cucumber slices and a mint sprig.

« WITH A TWIST

- 35ml (2 generous tablespoons) Sipsmith London Dry Gin
- 3 teaspoons dry vermouth
- 2 lemon wedges
- Small bunch of mint leaves
- Fever-Tree Cucumber Tonic Water, to top up
- 3 thin cucumber slices, to garnish

Pour the gin and vermouth into a cocktail shaker full of ice cubes. Squeeze over the lemon wedges, then discard the shells. Add the mint leaves. Shake for 15 seconds, then pour the contents of the shaker into a copa or wine glass. Top up with the tonic water. Garnish with the cucumber slices.

SPICED CLEMENTINE

It may sound like a festive favourite, but this drink can be enjoyed all year round. The subtle sweetness of clementines is the perfect sparring partner for the hint of cinnamon in the tonic water, and the two come together with the exotic spices of Opihr Gin and rosemary to create a warm G&T with a surprisingly sweet edge.

»

- 50ml (2fl oz) Opihr Gin
- Fever-Tree Clementine Tonic Water, to top up
- Clementine or orange wedge, to garnish

Add the gin to a highball glass filled with ice cubes. Top up with the tonic water. Garnish with a clementine or orange wedge.

WITH A TWIST

- 30ml (2 tablespoons) Opihr Gin
- 3 teaspoons Grand Marnier
- 2 clementine or orange wedges, plus an extra wedge to garnish
- Fever-Tree Clementine Tonic Water, to top up
- Small rosemary sprig, to garnish

Add the gin and Grand Marnier to a highball glass filled with ice cubes. Squeeze over the clementine or orange wedges, then discard the shells. Top up with the tonic water. Garnish with an extra clementine or orange wedge and a small rosemary sprig.

RHUBARB & GINGER

Rhubarb and ginger are both subtly spicy and incredibly crisp – that's why they work so well together. This highball is a splendid showcase for both flavours, with sweet, crisp Warner's Rhubarb Gin mixing marvellously well with ginger ale and lemon for a long, tangy take on a classic G&T.

- 50ml (2fl oz) Warner's Rhubarb Gin
- 1 lemon, halved
- Fever-Tree Ginger Ale, to top up

Pour the gin into a highball glass filled with ice cubes. Squeeze over the lemon halves and discard. Top up with the ginger ale.

WITH A TWIST »

- 35ml (2 generous tablespoons) Warner's Rhubarb Gin
- 3 teaspoons sweet red vermouth
- 2 lemon wedges
- Fever-Tree Ginger Ale, to top up
- Long rhubarb slice or an extra lemon wedge, to garnish

Pour the gin into a highball glass filled with ice. Add the sweet vermouth. Squeeze over and then drop in the lemon wedges. Top up with the ginger ale. Garnish either with a long rhubarb slice or an extra lemon wedge squeezed over and then dropped into the glass.

> >>> If you don't have a rhubarb gin, you can use a premium gin instead and add 1 teaspoon of rhubarb or other fruit jam to replicate the flavour. Make sure you stir the drink gently but thoroughly so that the jam dissolves.

WILD BERRY

This simple drink strikes perfectly that delicate balance between sweet and sour. On the one hand, lemons and London Dry gin bring bitterness. On the other, fresh raspberries, sweet vermouth and fruity tonic water balance out the botanicals. The result is a mouth-watering, well-matched mix.

«

- 50ml (2fl oz) London Dry gin (we like Bombay Sapphire)
- Fever-Tree Sweet Rhubarb & Raspberry Tonic Water, to top up
- Raspberry, to garnish

Pour the gin into a copa or wine glass filled with ice cubes. Top up with the tonic water. Garnish with a fresh raspberry.

WITH A TWIST

- 35ml (2 generous tablespoons) London Dry gin
- 2 lemon wedges
- 25ml (5 teaspoons) sweet red vermouth
- Fever-Tree Sweet Rhubarb & Raspberry Tonic Water, to top up
- Raspberry, to garnish

Pour the gin into a copa or wine glass filled with ice cubes. Squeeze over and drop in the lemon wedges. Add the sweet vermouth. Top up with the tonic water. Garnish with a fresh raspberry.

SLOE GIN & LEMON TONIC

Sloes are the bitter fruit of the blackthorn bush. While sloe gin tempers this tartness with sugar, we'd argue that it adds too much sweetness. That's why, for this refreshing, reinvented G&T, we're adding some refreshing bitterness back – in the form of Fever-Tree Lemon Tonic Water.

- 50ml (2fl oz) Hayman's or Sipsmith Sloe Gin
- Fever-Tree Lemon Tonic Water, to top up
- Lemon wedge, to garnish

Add the sloe gin to a highball glass filled with ice cubes. Top up with the tonic water. Garnish with a lemon wedge.

WITH A TWIST »

- 50ml (2fl oz) Hayman's or Sipsmith Sloe Gin
- 2 lemon wedges
- Fever-Tree Lemon Tonic Water, to top up
- 25ml (5 teaspoons) red wine

Add the sloe gin to a cocktail shaker full of ice cubes. Squeeze over and drop in the lemon wedges. Shake for 15 seconds, then pour the contents of the shaker into a copa or wine glass. Top up with the tonic water and add the red wine.

>>> If you don't have any sloe gin, try making a berry gin of your own. To a half-full bottle of gin, add 250g (9oz) fresh berries of your choice and 100g (3½oz) sugar. Shake well, then leave to rest for a month or two, giving it another little shake once a week.

TEQUILA & CITRUS

Tonic isn't just for gin. This recipe takes tonic and mixes it with tequila, creating an exciting new drink experience. The lemon and quinine flavours of the tonic water hit the tequila head-on, working with its soft spices to produce a zingy and thoroughly modern cocktail.

- 50ml (2fl oz) Patrón Tequila
- Fever-Tree Citrus Tonic Water, to top up
- Lime wedge, to garnish

Pour the tequila into a highball glass filled with ice cubes. Top up with the tonic water. Garnish with a lime wedge.

« WITH A TWIST

- 35ml (2 generous tablespoons) Patrón Tequila
- 3 teaspoons Cointreau
- 2 teaspoons pineapple juice
- Fever-Tree Citrus Tonic Water, to top up
- Pineapple wedge and leaf, to garnish

Pour the tequila, Cointreau and pineapple juice into a cocktail shaker full of ice cubes. Shake for 15 seconds, then pour the contents of the shaker into a highball glass. Top up with the tonic water. Garnish with a pineapple wedge and a pineapple leaf.

>>> Fever-Tree Citrus Tonic Water is a product designed specifically for our US market, but readers outside the USA can replace it with our Lemon or Mediterranean Tonic Water.

SUMMER BREEZE

Vermouth is the gin of the wine world. Flavoured with herbs, roots and berries, it can put complex, unexpected spins on existing drinks. This cocktail is the perfect example – mixed with herb-infused tonic water and St-Germain elderflower liqueur, the often-sidelined fortified wine suddenly becomes the main attraction.

»

- 50ml (2fl oz) Lillet Blanc
- 1 lemon wedge, plus an extra wedge to garnish
- Fever-Tree Mediterranean Tonic Water, to top up
- Small rosemary sprig, to garnish

Pour the Lillet into a copa or wine glass filled with ice cubes. Squeeze over the lemon wedge, then discard the shell. Top up with the tonic water. Garnish with an extra lemon wedge and a small rosemary sprig.

WITH A TWIST

- 30ml (2 tablespoons) Lillet Blanc
- 20ml (4 teaspoons) St-Germain elderflower liqueur
- 1 lemon wedge
- Fever-Tree Mediterranean Tonic Water, to top up
- Apple slices, to garnish
- Small rosemary sprig, to garnish

Pour the Lillet and elderflower liqueur into an empty cocktail shaker. Squeeze over and then drop in the lemon wedge. Add plenty of ice cubes. Shake for 15 seconds, then pour the contents of the shaker into a copa glass. Top up with the tonic water. Garnish with apple slices and a small rosemary sprig.

>>> Martini Bianco Vermouth or Cinzano Bianco Vermouth would also work well here if you don't have any Lillet Blanc.

BOURBON & TONIC

Bourbon is sweeter than Scotch whisky, which means it brings a new dimension to cocktails. Rich and well-rounded, this drink is topped up with sweetly sharp Fever-Tree Lemon Tonic Water and introduces the fruity flavour of peach purée into the mix. The lemon gives the drink a bitter edge, making it taste like a longer, more refreshing Whisky Sour.

«

- 50ml (2fl oz) premium bourbon, such as Jim Beam
- Fever-Tree Lemon Tonic Water, to top up
- Twist of lemon peel, to garnish

Fill a highball glass to the brim with ice cubes and pour over the bourbon. Top up with the tonic water. Garnish with a twist of lemon peel.

WITH A TWIST

- 50ml (2fl oz) premium bourbon, such as Jim Beam
- 30ml (2 tablespoons) peach purée
- 1 lemon wedge
- Fever-Tree Lemon Tonic Water, to top up
- 25ml (5 teaspoons) red wine

Add the bourbon and peach pureé to a cocktail shaker full of ice cubes. Squeeze over and then drop in the lemon wedge. Shake well for 15 seconds. Pour the contents of the shaker into a highball glass, then top up with the tonic water. Pour the red wine over the top of the drink – this is for both flavour and visual effect.

> > > A little peach liqueur or 1 teaspoon of peach jam would also work here if you don't have any peach purée.

SODAS & SPRITZES

SODAS & SPRITZES

The spritz started life as the German 'spritzen' – a 'splash' or 'spray' of soda water added to wine by Austrian troops, stationed in modern-day Italy, who longed for the lower-strength beers of home. And the word could not better describe the drink's mood – a dash of ritzy sparkle and the bubbly hiss of a freshly cracked soda. It is the sound of good times, with an accompanying backing track of laughter and fine conversation.

Today, the spritz most commonly appears as a combination of wine, soda and a more bitter and savoury aperitif – like Campari, Cynar or Aperol. The Italians, of course, are the undisputed masters of the art. Up and down the peninsula, the spritzy *aperitivo* hour is as sacred a ritual as their *sprezzatura* dressing or their morning coffee. It is estimated that around 300,000 spritzes are served daily in Venice alone.

As more and more of us make the move to longer, lighter and more refreshing drinks, the lower-calorie spritz serve has truly come into its own. Naturally, at Fever-Tree, we have endeavoured to produce the perfect partners for these classic drinks, using the very finest ingredients from the Mediterranean and beyond. Our Italian Blood Orange Soda, for example, contains oranges picked from a tiny area to the south of Mount Etna, where the colder winters bring out a darker, richer blush in the fruit's juicy flesh. Finally, our Sparkling Pink Grapefruit is full of juicy, tangy, sweet fruits from subtropical Florida that are picked just once a year, at peak ripeness. A combination of real juice and refreshing carbonation, these sodas are the perfect evocation of the modern spritz – light, bubbly, delicious and filled with sunshine.

Meanwhile, the classic vodka, lime and soda needed a spritz-up. While the world of vodka has become ever more premium and focused on the craft and provenance of its liquid, the lime part of the drink has been left behind and indeed has very little to do with limes themselves. So we searched the globe for two amazing citrus fruit – yuzu from Japan and Persian limes from the Yucatán Peninsula of Mexico – to make the ultimate lime soda, with the all-important carbonation to deliver these wonderful flavours. Consequently, with our Mexican Lime Soda, we have perfected another well-loved classic, just like we did with the G&T.

ULTIMATE VODKA LIME SODA

With a simple drink, the important thing is to mix confidently and use the finest ingredients. This vibrant Vodka & Lime Soda swaps out sugary cordial for real fruit, lime and yuzu soda and a refreshing mint sprig. Paired with clean Grey Goose Vodka, this makes for the best version ever of this classic cocktail.

«

- 50ml (2fl oz) Grey Goose Vodka
- Fever-Tree Mexican Lime Soda, to top up
- Lime wedge, to garnish
- Mint sprig, to garnish

Pour the vodka into a highball glass filled with ice cubes. Top up with the soda. Garnish with a lime wedge and a mint sprig.

WITH A TWIST

- 35ml (2 generous tablespoons) Grey Goose Vodka
- 3 teaspoons dry vermouth
- 2 lime wedges
- 3 cucumber slices
- Fever-Tree Mexican Lime Soda, to top up
- Apple wedge, to garnish

Pour the vodka and vermouth into a cocktail shaker filled with plenty of ice cubes. Squeeze over and then drop in the lime wedges and add the cucumber slices. Shake for 15 seconds, then pour the contents of the shaker into a highball glass. Top up with the soda. Garnish with an apple wedge.

>>> Don't forget to slap the mint leaves a little to release their aromas (see page 12).

LONG COSMOPOLITAN

This fresh, fruity twist on a classic cocktail is packed with vibrant, full-bodied flavours. Vodka, cranberry juice and Cointreau create a sweet base, and the soda, with its Mexican lime essence and Japanese yuzu extract, adds the perfect finishing touch. Fresh orange contributes an extra touch of sharpness to bring everything together.

»

- 35ml (2 generous tablespoons) premium vodka (we like Belvedere)
- 3 teaspoons Cointreau
- 25ml (5 teaspoons) cranberry juice
- Fever-Tree Mexican Lime Soda, to top up
- Lime wedge, to garnish

Fill a tall glass with ice cubes. Pour over the vodka, Cointreau and cranberry juice. Top up with the soda. Garnish with a lime wedge.

WITH A TWIST

- 35ml (2 generous tablespoons) premium vodka
- 3 teaspoons Cointreau
- 25ml (5 teaspoons) cranberry juice
- 3 teaspoons Lillet Rosé or Martini Rosato Vermouth, or any rosé vermouth
- Fever-Tree Mexican Lime Soda, to top up
- 1 orange wedge

Fill a tall glass with ice cubes. Pour over the vodka, Cointreau and cranberry juice. Add the rosé vermouth – this will add undertones of strawberry and raspberry that will complement the flavour of the drink. Top up with the soda. Squeeze the orange wedge over and then drop it into the glass to garnish.

LONG MARGARITA

When done well, Mexico's most famous cocktail balances the four primary categories of taste. This longer twist on the classic drink starts with salt and chilli to even out the sweetness of the Cointreau and agave syrup. A crisp lime wedge serves up a sour tang. Finally, Patrón Reposado Tequila brings bitterness to complete the experience.

- 35ml (2 generous tablespoons) Patrón Reposado Tequila
- 3 teaspoons Cointreau
- Fever-Tree Mexican Lime Soda, to top up
- Lime wedge, to garnish

Pour the tequila into a highball glass filled with ice cubes. Add the Cointreau. Top up with the soda. Garnish with a lime wedge.

≪ WITH A TWIST

- 2:1 mix of sea salt and dried chilli flakes
- 35ml (2 generous tablespoons) Patrón Reposado Tequila
- 3 teaspoons Cointreau
- 2 teaspoons agave syrup
- 2 teaspoons fresh lime juice, plus a lime wedge to garnish
- Fever-Tree Mexican Lime Soda, to top up

Frost the rim of a highball or rocks glass with the sea salt and chilli flake mix (see Tip below). Pour the tequila, Cointreau, agave syrup and lime juice into an empty cocktail shaker. Add plenty of ice cubes and shake vigorously for 15 seconds. Pour the contents of the shaker into your prepared glass. Top up with the soda. Garnish with a lime wedge.

> >>> To add a frosted rim, dip the rim of your glass in a saucer of lime or lemon juice or water. Spread 2 parts sea salt to 1 part dried chilli flakes on a small plate and place the rim of the glass in the frosting. Twist to give an even coating.

PALOMA

Created in the Mexican town of Tequila, this classic cocktail is a tangy Mexican masterpiece. For a twist, add Campari and agave syrup. It sounds like it should be spicy, but the savoury sea salt and fresh grapefruit, mixed with Fever-Tree Sparkling Pink Grapefruit, give it a gentle finish.

- 50ml (2fl oz) Patrón Tequila
- Fever-Tree Sparkling Pink Grapefruit, to top up
- Pink grapefruit wedge, to garnish

Pour the tequila into a highball glass filled with ice cubes. Top up with the sparkling pink grapefruit. Garnish with a pink grapefruit wedge.

« WITH A TWIST

- Sea salt
- 40ml (1¼fl oz) Patrón Tequila
- 2 teaspoons Campari
- 1 teaspoon agave syrup
- 2 lime wedges
- Fever-Tree Sparkling Pink Grapefruit, to top up
- Pink grapefruit wedge, to garnish

Frost the rim of a highball glass with the salt (see Tip, page 67). Pour the tequila, Campari and agave syrup into a cocktail shaker filled with ice cubes. Squeeze over and then drop in the lime wedges. Shake for 15 seconds. Fill your prepared glass with a few more ice cubes, then pour the contents of the shaker into the glass. Top up with the sparkling pink grapefruit. Garnish with a pink grapefruit wedge.

>>> If you can't get hold of Sparkling Pink Grapefruit, you can also create this drink with a splash of cranberry juice and our Sicilian Lemonade.

SMOKY PALOMA

This darker, richer spin on the Paloma is the perfect way to explore the smoky depths of tequila's smouldering cousin mezcal. We've chosen Vida Mezcal, as its aromatic, woody flavours mix particularly well with sharp lime and grapefruit additions. To top things off, agave syrup offers some subtle seasoning.

»

- 50ml (2fl oz) Vida Mezcal
- Fever-Tree Sparkling Pink Grapefruit or Lemon Tonic Water, to top up
- 2 limes, halved, with a wedge reserved to garnish

Pour the mezcal into a highball glass full of ice cubes. Top up with the pink grapefruit or tonic water. Squeeze over the lime halves and discard, then garnish with the reserved lime wedge.

WITH A TWIST

- 35ml (2 generous tablespoons) Vida Mezcal
- 3 teaspoons Cointreau
- 1 teaspoon agave syrup
- 1 pink grapefruit wedge, plus an extra wedge to garnish
- 2 limes
- Fever-Tree Sparkling Pink Grapefruit or Lemon Tonic Water, to top up

Fill a highball glass with ice cubes. Pour over the mezcal, Cointreau and agave syrup. Squeeze in the juice from the grapefruit wedge. Stir gently to make sure the agave syrup is mixed in. Top up with the pink grapefruit or tonic water. Halve the limes and squeeze in the juice. Garnish with a pink grapefruit wedge.

> >>> You can add a smoky twist to any tequila cocktail recipe by using a good-quality mezcal. And you can make this drink even smokier by adding a pinch of smoked sea salt, which really helps elevate the flavour.

TEXAS RANCH WATER

This Texan-style cocktail mixes lightly sweet Don Julio Tequila with spicy red chilli, cooling cucumber and a handful of herby basil to create a drink with fiery but floral depths. And to ensure it's not too spicy, we've added a double citrus serving of lime wedges and lime soda for a balanced finish.

》

- 50ml (2fl oz) Don Julio Tequila
- 1 red chilli, cut into 1-cm (½-inch) slices
- Fever-Tree Mexican Lime Soda, to top up
- Long cucumber ribbon, to garnish

Pour the tequila into a highball glass filled with ice cubes. Add the chilli slices. Top up with the soda. Garnish with a long cucumber ribbon curled around the inside of the glass.

WITH A TWIST

- 50ml (2fl oz) Don Julio Tequila
- 6 basil leaves
- 2 lime wedges
- Fever-Tree Mexican Lime Soda, to top up
- Long cucumber ribbon, to garnish

Add the tequila, basil leaves and lime wedges to an empty cocktail shaker. Add plenty of ice cubes and shake vigorously for 15 seconds. Pour the contents of the shaker into a highball glass. Top up with the soda. Garnish with a long cucumber ribbon curled around the inside of the glass.

>>> To cut an attractive ribbon of cucumber, use a vegetable peeler to peel a long slice from one end of a whole cucumber to the other.

VODKA PINK GRAPEFRUIT

It's hard to believe, but this simple, colourful drink tastes even better than it looks. The refreshingly crisp Grey Goose Vodka is infused with the fresh flavours of strawberry and basil – and a shot of striking, bittersweet Aperol gives the whole glass a sparklingly orange, thoroughly summery glow.

- 50ml (2fl oz) Grey Goose Vodka
- Fever-Tree Sparkling Pink Grapefruit, to top up
- Thin pink grapefruit slice, to garnish

Pour the vodka into a copa or wine glass filled with ice cubes. Top up with the sparkling pink grapefruit. Garnish with a thin slice of pink grapefruit.

« WITH A TWIST

- 40ml (1¼fl oz) Grey Goose Vodka
- 2 teaspoons Aperol
- 1 strawberry, sliced, plus extra slices to garnish
- 2 basil leaves, torn into small pieces
- Fever-Tree Sparkling Pink Grapefruit, to top up

Add the vodka and Aperol to an empty cocktail shaker. Add the sliced strawberry, basil leaves and plenty of ice cubes. Shake for 15 seconds. Pour the contents of the shaker into a copa or wine glass. Top up with the sparkling pink grapefruit. Garnish with strawberry slices.

>>> If you can't get hold of Sparkling Pink Grapefruit, you can also create this drink with a splash of cranberry juice and our Sicilian Lemonade.

VODKA & ITALIAN BLOOD ORANGE

Citrus doesn't always have to be sour. This simple drink embraces the well-rounded natural flavours of rich, juicy oranges and aromatic herbs. Together, the combination creates a sweetness even the zesty lemon garnish can't take away.

»

- 50ml (2fl oz) Ketel One Vodka
- Fever-Tree Italian Blood Orange Soda, to top up
- Twist of lemon peel, to garnish

Add the vodka to a copa or wine glass filled with ice cubes. Top up with the soda. Garnish with a twist of lemon peel.

WITH A TWIST

- 4 raspberries
- 35ml (2 generous tablespoons) Ketel One Vodka
- 3 teaspoons Aperol
- 1 lemon wedge, plus a long twist of lemon peel to garnish
- Fever-Tree Italian Blood Orange Soda, to top up

Muddle (or crush) the raspberries in the bottom of your copa or wine glass, then add ice cubes on top. Pour over the vodka and Aperol. Squeeze over the lemon wedge, then discard the shell. Top up with the soda. Garnish with a long twist of lemon peel.

>>> If you don't have fresh raspberries, you can replace them with a little raspberry liqueur or 1 teaspoon of raspberry jam. Make sure you stir the drink gently but thoroughly so that the jam dissolves. This drink works well mixed in a cocktail shaker too.

CAMPARI SPRITZ

Campari is one of the world's most famous aperitifs and it plays an important part in many classic cocktails. Here, the liqueur partners up with blood orange soda, Tanqueray's bittersweet, botanical Flor de Sevilla Gin and sweet vermouth to create a spritz bursting with refreshing citrus flavours.

«

- 50ml (2fl oz) Campari
- Fever-Tree Italian Blood Orange Soda, to top up
- Orange wedge, to garnish

Add the Campari to a copa or wine glass filled with ice cubes. Top up with the soda. Garnish with an orange wedge.

WITH A TWIST

- 25ml (5 teaspoons) Campari
- 25ml (5 teaspoons) Tanqueray Flor de Sevilla Gin
- 25ml (5 teaspoons) sweet red vermouth
- Fever-Tree Italian Blood Orange Soda, to top up
- Long twist of orange peel, to garnish

Pour the Campari, gin and vermouth into a tall glass filled with ice cubes. Stir gently until combined. Add a few more ice cubes, then top up with the soda. Garnish with a long twist of orange peel, curled around the inside of the glass, to add a delicate citrus aroma.

>>> Did you know that blood oranges only blush when exposed to sub-zero temperatures on the tree? The colder the winter, the redder the fruit.

ELDERFLOWER GIN SPRITZ

The main purpose of a spritz is to invigorate the drinker. But it's also meant to give you an appetite. This spritz, a wonderfully fresh mix of intensely aromatic Pink Pepper Gin, juicy Cointreau and our floral Elderflower Tonic Water, does both jobs beautifully. And don't skimp on the mint – it's essential for the full experience.

«

- 35ml (2 generous tablespoons) Pink Pepper Gin
- 3 teaspoons Cointreau
- 3 lemon wedges, plus a twist of lemon peel to garnish
- Fever-Tree Elderflower Tonic Water, to top up
- Mint sprig, to garnish

Add the gin and Cointreau to a copa glass filled with ice cubes. Squeeze over and then drop in the lemon wedges. Top up with the tonic water. Garnish with a twist of lemon peel and a fresh mint sprig.

WITH A TWIST

- 35ml (2 generous tablespoons) Pink Pepper Gin
- 3 teaspoons Cointreau
- 3 lemon wedges, plus a twist of lemon peel to garnish
- Mint sprig, plus extra leaves to garnish
- Fever-Tree Elderflower Tonic Water, to top up

Add the gin and Cointreau to an empty cocktail shaker. Squeeze over and then drop in the lemon wedges. Add the mint sprig and plenty of ice cubes. Shake vigorously for 15 seconds. Pour the contents of the shaker into a copa or wine glass. Top up with the tonic water. Garnish with a twist of lemon peel and fresh mint leaves.

CUCUMBER WINE SPRITZ

Wines made with Sauvignon Blanc grapes are packed with the tart flavours of green apples and gooseberries. These sharp notes work particularly well with refreshing Fever-Tree Cucumber Tonic Water and St-Germain elderflower liqueur in this sparkling spritz, creating one of the lightest, brightest drinks in this book.

- 60ml (4 tablespoons) white wine (we like Sauvignon Blanc)
- Fever-Tree Cucumber Tonic Water, to top up
- Lemon wedge, to garnish
- Cucumber slice, to garnish

Pour the white wine into a highball glass filled with ice cubes. Top up with the tonic water. Garnish with a lemon wedge and a cucumber slice.

WITH A TWIST »

- 60ml (4 tablespoons) white wine
- 3 teaspoons St-Germain elderflower liqueur
- Fever-Tree Cucumber Tonic Water, to top up
- Lemon wedge, to garnish
- Cucumber ribbon, to garnish

For a refreshing, easy cocktail, pour the white wine into a highball glass filled with ice cubes. Add the elderflower liqueur – a wonderful addition to the cucumber flavours here. Top up with the tonic water. Garnish with a lemon wedge and a cucumber ribbon.

WILD BERRY SPRITZ

This deep, well-rounded drink sees berries and bubbles come together in sweet harmony to create a rich, sparkling spritz. Juicy Aperol and prosecco kick the cocktail off, offering a vibrant combination of bubbly, syrupy textures. Fruity tonic tops it off decadently with a light, frothy fizz.

»

- 50ml (2fl oz) Aperol
- 50ml (2fl oz) prosecco
- Fever-Tree Sweet Rhubarb & Raspberry Tonic Water, to top up

Add the Aperol and prosecco to a copa or wine glass filled with ice cubes. Top up with the tonic water.

WITH A TWIST

- 50ml (2fl oz) Aperol
- 2 lemon wedges
- 6 raspberries, plus 2 extra to garnish
- 50ml (2fl oz) prosecco
- Fever-Tree Sweet Rhubarb & Raspberry Tonic Water, to top up

Pour the Aperol into an empty cocktail shaker. Squeeze over and then drop in the lemon wedges. Add the raspberries and plenty of ice cubes. Shake vigorously for 15 seconds, then pour the contents of the shaker into a copa or wine glass. Top up with the prosecco and tonic water. Garnish with the extra raspberries.

>>> If you don't have any raspberries, you can add 1 teaspoon of raspberry jam to the cocktail shaker instead.

WHITE GRAPE & APRICOT SPRITZ

There's something to be said for subtlety. This cocktail may sound busy, but its understated ingredients offer gentle, fruity flavours. Fever-Tree White Grape & Apricot Soda blends in especially smoothly with the Martini Bianco Vermouth and Chambord or crème de mûre to create a delicious and delicate sipper.

- 30ml (2 tablespoons) Martini Bianco Vermouth
- 20ml (4 teaspoons) Chambord or crème de mûre
- Fever-Tree White Grape & Apricot Soda, to top up
- Apricot slice, to garnish
- Blackberry, to garnish

Fill a highball glass with ice cubes. Pour over the vermouth and the Chambord or crème de mûre. Stir gently to mix. Top up with the soda. Garnish with an apricot slice and a blackberry.

« WITH A TWIST

- A handful of frozen berries (raspberries, blackberries, strawberries and/or redcurrants)
- 30ml (2 tablespoons) Lillet Blanc or sweet white vermouth
- 20ml (4 teaspoons) Chambord or crème de mûre
- Fever-Tree White Grape & Apricot Soda, to top up
- A few fresh berries, to garnish

Add a handful of frozen berries to a highball glass, then add ice cubes. Pour in the Lillet or vermouth and the Chambord or crème de mûre. Top up with the soda. Garnish with a few fresh berries of your choice.

>>> You can use fresh berries instead of frozen berries here, but frozen ones will thaw slowly, releasing fresh juice into the drink as they do so, giving it an evolving flavour.

MULES &
MOJITOS

MULES & MOJITOS

As with many great inventions, the precise origin of the Moscow Mule is fiercely disputed. But it seems most likely that the eureka moment occurred at some point in the 1940s, down in the cellar of an English-style pub on Hollywood's Sunset Strip. John Martin, the then-importer of a fledgling vodka brand named Smirnoff, had given a case of the spirit to his barman friend Jack Morgan. For months the case sat underground, unused, gathering dust next to a lonely crate of surplus ginger beer. Until one day, in an effort to clear out the cluttered basement, head barman Wes Price mixed up a simple concoction of vodka, ginger beer and a squeeze of lime, and served it to an actor named Broderick Crawford, and the rest, as they say, is history. 'I was just trying to get rid of a lot of dead stock,' Price would later say. 'But it caught on like wildfire.'

The drink is still in the pink now. The Mule (in all its many glorious variations) is today a staple of bar menus and home repertoires the world over. Our ginger beer is the perfect partner, with its full-bodied mix of three unique variants of the root: fresh green ginger from the Ivory Coast, with its distinctive lemon grass zestiness; Nigerian ginger, full of aromatic intensity and characteristic spice; and Cochin ginger from India – warm, deep and well-rounded. We feel it gives the Mule its requisite kick and warming tail-wag – and adds to this great drink's rollicking heritage.

While ginger beer is something that has been brewed for centuries in England, ginger ale was invented much more recently, originating in Belfast just over 150 years ago. Our ginger ale is made in a slightly different way to our ginger beer. Instead of brewing all the ginger roots together, we harvest, wash and then distill each separate ginger in the location where it is grown, and the essential oil we gather from each is then blended together to create a balanced flavour, very much like whisky makers do to create their famous blends. As we use only the oils, our ginger ale doesn't carry quite the same heat as our ginger beer, and the liquid isn't cloudy.

For sheer popularity and beautiful simplicity, the Mule is perhaps only matched by the Mojito – that dazzling dance of citrus, mint, rum and soda. The Mojito's origins are even less certain than that of the Mule – a bar called La Bodeguita in Havana, Cuba, proudly claims ownership of the recipe (its version was championed by the ever-watered Ernest Hemingway in a famous act of graffiti), while others say the concoction dates back to the 1500s and explorer Sir Francis Drake.

When the ingredients are this harmonious, however, the inventor doesn't much matter. At Fever-Tree, we like to lift the Classic Mojito with a decent measure of our Mexican Lime Soda – crafted with Persian lime from Mexico's fragrant citrus groves and a pressed oil extract from the floral Japanese yuzu fruit. We like to imagine Hemingway would approve.

RASPBERRY MULE

This recipe, which introduces Chambord liqueur to a classic Mule, gives the traditional cocktail a fruity edge. The tang of the raspberries matches the bite of the ginger, and the fresh lime gives the drink a clean, crisp and thoroughly refreshing finish.

- 35ml (2 generous tablespoons) premium vodka (we like Grey Goose)
- 3 teaspoons Chambord
- Fever-Tree Ginger Beer, to top up
- 2 lime wedges
- 2 raspberries, to garnish
- Mint sprig, to garnish

Fill a copper or glass mug with ice cubes and pour over the vodka and Chambord. Top up with the ginger beer. Squeeze over and then drop in the lime wedges. Garnish with the raspberries and a mint sprig.

« WITH A TWIST

- 5 or 6 mint leaves, plus an extra sprig to garnish
- 3 raspberries, plus an extra raspberry to garnish
- 40ml (1¼fl oz) premium vodka
- 20ml (4 teaspoons) Chambord
- Fever-Tree Ginger Beer, to top up
- Mint sprig, to garnish
- Dark chocolate, for grating to garnish (optional)

Add the mint leaves and raspberries to an empty cocktail shaker. Pour in the vodka and Chambord and add plenty of ice cubes. Shake vigorously for 15 seconds. Pour the contents of the shaker into a copper or glass mug and add a couple more ice cubes. Top up with the ginger beer. Garnish with an extra raspberry and a mint sprig. For a touch of decadence, you can grate a little dark chocolate over the raspberry.

PINEAPPLE MULE

The Mule may be most closely associated with chilly Moscow, but this tropical twist adds sun-soaked spirit to the famous cocktail. By pouring in a generous measure of sweet pineapple juice, adding a squeeze of fresh lime and garnishing with mint leaves, an exquisitely exotic spin on a traditional recipe is created.

»

- 50ml (2fl oz) premium vodka (we like Smirnoff)
- 50ml (2fl oz) pineapple juice
- Fever-Tree Ginger Beer, to top up
- 1 lime wedge
- Mint sprigs, to garnish

Fill a highball glass with ice cubes, then pour over the vodka and the pineapple juice. Add a couple more ice cubes and top up with the ginger beer. Squeeze over and then drop in the lime wedge. Garnish with mint.

WITH A TWIST

- 50ml (2fl oz) premium vodka
- 50ml (2fl oz) pineapple juice
- 2 pineapple slices
- A pinch of salt
- Fever-Tree Ginger Beer, to top up
- Long pineapple leaf, to garnish

Pour the vodka and pineapple juice into an empty cocktail shaker. Add the pineapple slices and a pinch of salt. Top up with ice cubes. Shake vigorously for 15 seconds, then pour the contents of the shaker into a highball glass. Top up with the ginger beer. Finally, take a long pineapple leaf and slide it down inside the glass to garnish.

>>> This drink would also work really well with dark rum instead of the vodka.

WATERMELON MULE

Bright pink, fiercely fresh and dripping with soft, sweet flavour, watermelon is the perfect addition to the classic Mule. It not only brings out the natural brightness of the mint and the cooling quality of the lime, it also bubbles up through the vodka and peppery Fever-Tree Ginger Beer so that every sip fizzes with flavour.

«

- 50ml (2fl oz) premium vodka (we like Ketel One)
- 2 watermelon cubes (deseeded), plus extra to garnish
- Fever-Tree Ginger Beer, to top up
- 2 lime wedges
- Mint sprig, to garnish

Fill a highball glass with ice cubes. Pour over the vodka. Add the watermelon cubes and a couple more ice cubes. Stir gently to agitate the fruit. Top up with the ginger beer. Squeeze over and then drop in the lime wedges. Garnish with a mint sprig and extra watermelon cubes.

WITH A TWIST

- 50ml (2fl oz) premium vodka
- 50g (1¾fl oz) watermelon cubes (deseeded), plus a large slice to garnish
- 3 lime wedges
- 1 teaspoon sugar syrup (see page 15)
- 5 or 6 mint leaves
- Fever-Tree Ginger Beer, to top up

Add the vodka and watermelon cubes to an empty cocktail shaker. Squeeze over and then drop in the lime wedges. Add the sugar syrup, the mint leaves and a scoop of ice cubes. Shake vigorously for 15 seconds, then pour the contents of the shaker into a copper or glass mug. Top up with a couple more ice cubes and the ginger beer. Garnish with a large watermelon slice.

COCONUT MULE

This cocktail combines fresh and creamy ingredients to excellent effect. The tartness of the lime and the sharpness of the ginger beer blend easily with the creamy coconut and well-rounded rums to mix a Mule of a different breed.

»

- 30ml (2 tablespoons) gold rum (we like Bacardí Reserva Ocho 8 Year Old Rum)
- 20ml (4 teaspoons) coconut rum
- Fever-Tree Ginger Beer, to top up
- 1 lime wedge

Fill a copper or glass mug with ice cubes. Pour over the golden rum and coconut rum. Top up with the ginger beer. Squeeze over and then drop in the lime wedge as a garnish.

WITH A TWIST

- 50ml (2fl oz) gold rum
- 2 teaspoons coconut cream
- 50ml (2fl oz) pineapple juice
- Fever-Tree Ginger Beer, to top up
- Lime wheel, to garnish

Add the gold rum, coconut cream and pineapple juice to an empty cocktail shaker. Add a good scoop of ice cubes, then shake vigorously for 15 seconds. Pour the contents of the shaker into a copper or glass mug and top up with the ginger beer. Garnish with a lime wheel.

DARK & STORMY

This world-famous cocktail was invented over two centuries ago by sailors who named it after the dark colour of dangerous skies. We've mixed a drink with a brighter outlook – complete with glimmers of sharp lime, flickers of sparkling ginger beer and a sweet, spiced tot of Gosling's Black Seal Rum.

«

- 50ml (2fl oz) Gosling's Black Seal Rum
- Fever-Tree Ginger Beer, to top up
- Lime wedge, to garnish

Fill a highball glass with ice cubes. Pour over the rum and top up with the ginger beer. Garnish with a lime wedge.

WITH A TWIST

- 35ml (2 generous tablespoons) Gosling's Black Seal Rum
- 35ml (2 generous tablespoons) Pedro Ximénez Sherry
- 3 drops Angostura Bitters
- 3 lime wedges, plus 2 extra wedges to garnish
- Fever-Tree Ginger Beer, to top up

Pour the rum into a highball glass filled with ice cubes. Add the sherry and the bitters. Top up the glass with a couple more ice cubes. Squeeze over the lime wedges, then discard the shells. Top up with the ginger beer. Garnish with the extra lime wedges.

KENTUCKY MULE

Kentucky is known around the world for its quality whiskey.
For this drink, use only the best bourbon, to lay a flavoursome
foundation for crisp ice, zesty lime and warming ginger beer.
Served with a dash of juicy peach and refreshing mint, this
southern spirit shines its rich, golden best.

»

- 50ml (2fl oz) premium bourbon (we like Jim Beam)
- 2 lime wedges
- Fever-Tree Ginger Beer, to top up

Pour the bourbon into a glass or copper mug filled with ice cubes.
Squeeze over and then drop in the lime wedges. Top up with the
ginger beer.

WITH A TWIST

- 35ml (2 generous tablespoons) premium bourbon
- 3 teaspoons peach liqueur
- 2 lime wedges
- Fever-Tree Ginger Beer, to top up
- Mint sprig, to garnish

Add the bourbon and the peach liqueur to a copper or glass mug filled with ice cubes.
Squeeze over and then drop in the lime wedges. Top up with the ginger beer.
Garnish with a mint sprig.

>>> You can replace the peach liqueur with a little peach purée or 1 teaspoon of peach jam if you
like. Make sure you stir the drink gently but thoroughly so that the purée or jam dissolves. If
you do this, you'll need to increase your bourbon measure to 50ml (2fl oz).

GIN BASIL MULE

Basil usually blends into the background or is used only as a last-minute garnish. In this cocktail, the herb is given its well-deserved time in the spotlight. Fresh lemon brings out the brightness of the basil and earthy Fever-Tree Ginger Beer creates a long drink with delicious basil-soaked depths.

- 50ml (2fl oz) Aviation Gin
- 2 lemon wedges
- Fever-Tree Ginger Beer, to top up
- Basil sprig, to garnish

Add the gin to a copper or glass mug filled with ice cubes. Squeeze over and then drop in the lemon wedges. Top up with the ginger beer. Garnish with a basil sprig.

« WITH A TWIST

- 35ml (2 generous tablespoons) Aviation Gin
- 12 basil leaves, plus an extra sprig to garnish
- 25ml (5 teaspoons) sweet white vermouth
- 2 lemon wedges
- Fever-Tree Ginger Beer, to top up

Pour the gin into an empty cocktail shaker. Tear the basil leaves gently to release their natural oils and flavours and add them to the shaker. Add the vermouth. Squeeze over and then drop in the lemon wedges. Fill the shaker with ice cubes, then shake vigorously for 15 seconds. Pour the contents of the shaker into a copper or glass mug. Top up with the ginger beer. Garnish with a basil sprig.

> > > Did you know that 'bianco' on a vermouth label is a reference to the white vanilla flowers it contains?

STRAWBERRY GIN MULE

Strawberry and spice are a flavour match made in cocktail heaven. From the tones of the fiery ginger beer and the piquant black pepper to the distinctive botanicals of Tanqueray's famous No. Ten Gin, the selection of spices in this drink are tempered – but not weakened – by the sweet juiciness of the strawberries.

»

- 1 teaspoon strawberry jam
- 50ml (2fl oz) Tanqueray No. Ten Gin
- 3 lemon wedges
- Fever-Tree Ginger Beer, to top up
- Strawberry slices, to garnish

Place the strawberry jam in the bottom of a copa or wine glass. Add the gin. Squeeze over the lemon wedges, then discard the shells. Fill the glass with ice cubes and stir well. Top up with the ginger beer. Garnish with strawberry slices.

WITH A TWIST

- 2 strawberries, cut into quarters, plus extra slices to garnish
- 50ml (2fl oz) Tanqueray No. Ten Gin
- 10 mint leaves, plus extra to garnish
- 2 teaspoons sugar syrup (see page 15)
- A twist of black pepper
- 2 lemon wedges
- Fever-Tree Ginger Beer, to top up

Place the strawberries in an empty cocktail shaker. Add the gin, mint leaves, sugar syrup and black pepper. Squeeze over and then drop in the lemon wedges. Top up with ice cubes and shake vigorously for 15 seconds. Pour the contents of the shaker into a copa or wine glass and add a couple more ice cubes. Top up with the ginger beer and garnish with extra strawberry slices and mint leaves.

AMARETTO MULE

In theory, almonds and ginger shouldn't work well together. The nuts are bitter, the spice is peppery and the tastes, presumably, incompatible. But this Amaretto Mule, a drink that introduces the almond-soaked spirit to fiery Fever-Tree Ginger Beer, is a pleasant, refreshing surprise. Expect sweet flavours, sharp lemon and a rich chocolaty finish.

- 50ml (2fl oz) Disaronno Amaretto
- Fever-Tree Ginger Beer, to top up
- 2 lemon wedges, to garnish

Fill a copper or glass mug with plenty of ice cubes. Pour over the amaretto. Top up with the ginger beer. Garnish with the lemon wedges.

« WITH A TWIST

- 25ml (5 teaspoons) Disaronno Amaretto
- 25ml (5 teaspoons) premium Cognac
- 2 lemon wedges
- Fever-Tree Ginger Beer, to top up
- Dark chocolate, grated, to garnish
- Nutmeg, grated, to garnish

Pour the amaretto and Cognac into an empty cocktail shaker. Squeeze over and then drop in the lemon wedges. Top up with ice cubes. Shake vigorously for 15 seconds, then pour into a glass or copper mug. Add a couple more ice cubes. Top up with the ginger beer. Garnish with grated dark chocolate and freshly grated nutmeg.

JÄGER MULE

There are over 50 different herbs and spices involved in the creation of Jägermeister. One of them is ginger. We've used this icy drink to tease out the natural notes of the root in the iconic German digestif. And when the Fever-Tree Ginger Beer fizzes its way to meet Jägermeister's botanicals, the flavours explode!

»

- 50ml (2fl oz) Jägermeister
- Fever-Tree Ginger Beer, to top up
- 3 lime wedges

Fill a highball glass with ice cubes, then pour over the Jägermeister. Top up with the ginger beer. Squeeze over the lime wedges, then drop them into the glass.

WITH A TWIST

- 10 mint leaves
- 50ml (2fl oz) Jägermeister
- Juice of ½ lime, plus a lime wedge to garnish
- Fever-Tree Ginger Beer, to top up

Tear the mint leaves gently to release their natural oils and place them in the bottom of a highball glass. Pour over the Jägermeister and the lime juice. Stir gently for a few seconds to allow the flavours to infuse. Fill the glass with ice cubes. Top up with the ginger beer. Stir again gently to ensure the ingredients are fully combined. Garnish with a lime wedge.

JALISCO MULE

Tequila and ginger are spicy soulmates. Distilled in the Jaliscan Highlands, Patrón Tequila has a natural peppery sweetness similar to the warm, zesty taste of ginger. This simple cocktail adds just a hint of bitter lime to the magnificent Mexican spirit. Stand back and let the fiery flavours dance!

«

- 50ml (2fl oz) Patrón Tequila
- Fever-Tree Ginger Beer, to top up
- Lime wedge, to garnish

Pour the tequila into a highball glass filled with ice cubes. Top up with the ginger beer. Garnish with a lime wedge.

WITH A TWIST

- 50ml (2fl oz) Patrón Tequila
- 2 lime wedges, plus an extra wedge to garnish
- 1 orange wedge
- Fever-Tree Ginger Beer, to top up

Add the tequila to an empty cocktail shaker. Squeeze over and then drop in the lime wedges and the orange wedge. Top up with ice cubes. Shake for 15 seconds. Pour the contents of the shaker into a highball glass. Top up with the ginger beer. Garnish with a lime wedge.

MEZCAL MULE

This spin on the classic Mule is a complex drink, balancing many different, distinct flavours. Mexican mezcal may be a smoky spirit, but it works well with the fresh ginger beer, lots of lime and a touch of basil. And it doesn't overpower the elderflower notes of the light, floral St-Germain liqueur. Each flavour simply enhances the next.

»

- 50ml (2fl oz) Vida Mezcal
- ½ lime, plus an extra wedge to garnish
- Fever-Tree Ginger Beer, to top up
- Basil sprig, to garnish

Pour the mezcal into a glass or copper mug filled with ice cubes. Squeeze over the lime half, then discard the shell. Top up with the ginger beer. Garnish with a lime wedge and a basil sprig.

WITH A TWIST

- 40ml (1¼fl oz) Vida Mezcal
- 20ml (4 teaspoons) St-Germain elderflower liqueur
- 3 lime wedges, plus an extra wedge to garnish
- Fever-Tree Ginger Beer, to top up
- Basil leaf, to garnish

Pour the mezcal and the elderflower liqueur into an empty cocktail shaker. Squeeze over and then drop in the lime wedges. Top up with ice cubes. Shake for 15 seconds, then pour the contents of the shaker into a tall glass. Top up with the ginger beer. Garnish with a lime wedge and a basil leaf.

CLASSIC MOJITO

One of the finest traditional cocktails that we all know and love, here the quintessential drink of Cuba fizzes with Fever-Tree's Mexican Lime Soda, adding a little more lime than usual to the bright white rum and vibrant mint of the classic recipe. Equal parts sharp and sweet, it's a lively, cool drink with a long, lingering finish.

«

- 10 mint leaves, plus extra mint to garnish
- 50ml (2fl oz) white rum (we like Bacardi)
- 2 teaspoons sugar syrup (see page 15)
- 2 lime wedges, plus an extra wedge to garnish
- Fever-Tree Mexican Lime Soda, to top up

Tear the mint leaves gently to release their natural oils and flavours. Place them in the bottom of a highball glass and fill up with ice cubes. Pour over the rum and the sugar syrup. Squeeze over the lime wedges, then discard the shells. Stir gently to mix the mint and the rum. Top up with the soda. Garnish with extra mint and a lime wedge.

WITH A TWIST

- A large handful of mint, plus an extra sprig to garnish
- 3 lime wedges, plus an extra wedge to garnish
- 2 teaspoons sugar syrup (see page 15)
- 50ml (2fl oz) white rum
- Fever-Tree Mexican Lime Soda, to top up

Add the mint to a cocktail shaker filled with ice cubes. Squeeze over the lime wedges. Pour over the sugar syrup and the rum. Shake vigorously for 15 seconds, then pour the contents into a highball glass. Top up with the soda. Garnish with a mint sprig and a lime wedge.

GIN MOJITO

The classic Mojito may be mixed with rum, but certain gins are also up to the job. Monkey 47 is one of them, distilled with the same spicy, grassy flavours that make rum such a perfect partner for mint and lime. This spin on the traditional cocktail also includes lemonade, for added sweetness.

»

- 10 mint leaves, plus an extra sprig to garnish
- 50ml (2fl oz) Monkey 47 Gin
- 2 teaspoons sugar syrup (see page 15)
- 2 lime wedges
- Fever-Tree Sicilian Lemonade, to top up
- Lemon wedge, to garnish

Tear the mint leaves gently to release their natural oils and flavours. Place them in the bottom of a copa or wine glass and fill up with ice cubes. Pour over the gin and the sugar syrup. Squeeze over the lime wedges, then discard the shells. Stir gently to mix the mint with the gin. Top up with the lemonade. Garnish with a mint sprig and a lemon wedge.

WITH A TWIST

- 50ml (2fl oz) Monkey 47 Gin
- 2 teaspoons sugar syrup (see page 15)
- 2 lime wedges, plus an extra wedge to garnish
- A large handful of mint leaves, plus an extra sprig to garnish
- Fever-Tree Sicilian Lemonade, to top up

Pour the gin and sugar syrup into an empty cocktail shaker. Squeeze over the lime wedges and add the mint leaves. Top up with ice cubes. Shake vigorously for 15 seconds, then pour the contents of the shaker into a copa or wine glass. Top up with the lemonade. Garnish with a mint sprig and a lime wedge.

GINGER MOJITO

Could ginger be the single elusive ingredient the classic Mojito has been missing? In this twist on the traditional cocktail, we've added the fizzy flavour of earthy root ginger to underscore both the zest of the lime and the zing of the fresh mint, creating an exciting, spicy spin on a timeless, refreshing classic.

- 10 mint leaves, plus an extra sprig to garnish
- 3 lime wedges
- 50ml (2fl oz) Havana Club Especial
- Fever-Tree Spiced Orange Ginger Ale, to top up
- Thin fresh root ginger slice, to garnish

Tear the mint leaves gently to release their natural oils and flavours. Place them in the bottom of a highball glass. Squeeze over and then drop in the lime wedges. Add the rum. Fill the glass with ice cubes and stir gently to mix well. Top up with the ginger ale. Garnish with a mint sprig and a thin fresh root ginger slice.

≪ WITH A TWIST

- A large handful of mint, plus an extra sprig to garnish
- ½ a lime, plus an extra wedge to garnish
- 2 teaspoons sugar syrup (see page 15)
- 50ml (2fl oz) Havana Club Especial
- Fever-Tree Spiced Orange Ginger Ale, to top up

Add the mint to an empty cocktail shaker. Squeeze over the ½ a lime, then discard the shell. Pour over the sugar syrup and the rum. Top up with plenty of ice cubes. Shake vigorously for 15 seconds, then pour the contents of the shaker into a highball glass. Top up with the ginger ale. Garnish with a mint sprig and a lime wedge.

RASPBERRY VODKA MOJITO

By using vodka in place of the rum, this twist on a traditional Mojito arguably creates a whole new cocktail. The clean qualities of vodka make it the perfect spirit for the Cuban classic. Vodka offers renewed freshness to the mint, crisps up the lemons and allows the sharp sweetness of the raspberries to shine through.

»

- 10 mint leaves, plus an extra sprig to garnish
- 1 lemon wedge
- 2 raspberries, plus an extra raspberry to garnish
- 50ml (2fl oz) premium vodka (we like Grey Goose)
- Fever-Tree Sicilian Lemonade, to top up

Tear the mint leaves gently to release their natural oils and flavours. Place them in the bottom of a highball glass. Squeeze over and then drop in the lemon wedge. Add the raspberries, then pour over the vodka. Fill the glass with ice cubes. Stir gently to mix well. Top up with the lemonade. Garnish with a mint sprig and a fresh raspberry.

WITH A TWIST

- A large handful of mint leaves, plus an extra sprig to garnish
- 3 raspberries
- 1 lemon wedge
- 2 teaspoons sugar syrup (see page 15)
- 50ml (2fl oz) premium vodka
- Fever-Tree Sicilian Lemonade, to top up

Add the mint leaves and raspberries to an empty cocktail shaker. Squeeze over and then drop in the lemon wedge. Pour over the sugar syrup and the vodka. Top up with plenty of ice cubes. Shake vigorously for 15 seconds, then pour the contents of the shaker into a highball glass. Top up with the lemonade. Garnish with a mint sprig.

HIGHBALLS & ODDBALLS

HIGHBALLS & ODDBALLS

Whisky is a drink almost mythical in its origins. *Usquaebach* is the ancient Gaelic word for 'water of life', and certainly the right sip of the right whisky at the right moment can be truly transcendental. This may explain the reverence that shrouds the drink, which can feel tricky to navigate – that shy and lingering fear, for example, of doing something sacrilegious with an ice cube. Aside from the usual 'Which tonic goes best with which gin?', the question most often asked of us at Fever-Tree is a nervous 'Am I allowed to mix whisky?' And the answer, we don't mind telling you, is an emphatic 'Yes!'

Don't just take our word for it though. On a recent trip to the Johnnie Walker headquarters in Scotland, our co-founder Tim was told by the master blender that he always keeps soda and ginger ale in his blending room. This allows the esteemed marque to establish precisely how each dram will work in a highball – the drink that has become the gold standard of mixed whisky.

The word 'highball' is often said to derive from an old railway term – a reference to the floating ball gauge indicator inside a steam train's water tank. When the ball was pumped high, the train was ready to depart – a pleasing metaphor for the enlivening effect of the first drink of the evening. Choo choo!

It's been full steam ahead since then. Today, the right combination of whisky and soda is a very special alchemy, emphasizing certain notes in the spirit while lending new depth and warmth to the mixer. We have included some winning examples here, including the elegant Japanese Highball and the hearty Irish variant. We've also found room at the end of the chapter for some weird and wonderful long-drink 'oddballs', discovered on our travels over the years. Remember – rules are there to be broken.

JAPANESE HIGHBALL

The Japanese Highball is a drink of zen-like simplicity. It celebrates the perfect union of rich Nikka Days Whisky and sparkling soda water in a long, balanced and thoroughly refreshing cocktail. We've introduced a drop of kirsch and a twist of lemon to give it a sweet and sour finish.

«

- 50ml (2fl oz) Nikka Days Whisky
- Fever-Tree Soda Water, to top up
- Twist of lemon peel, to garnish

Simply pour the whisky into a highball glass filled with ice cubes. Top up with the soda water. Garnish with a twist of lemon peel.

WITH A TWIST

- 50ml (2fl oz) Nikka Days Whisky
- 1 cherry from a jar, plus 1 teaspoon kirsch from the jar
- Fever-Tree Soda Water, to top up
- Twist of lemon peel, to garnish

Pour the whisky into a highball glass filled with ice cubes. Add a cherry and the kirsch from the jar. Top up with the soda water. Garnish with a twist of lemon peel.

>>> Did you know that the highball was the saviour of the Japanese whisky industry? Japanese whisky is now rightly regarded as one of the best in the world.

BOURBON HIGHBALL

This tall, fortifying drink introduces a touch of smoke to the sweet whiskey highball. Jim Beam's spin on vanilla and oak is immediately soaked up by the charred, woody bubbles of Fever-Tree Smoky Ginger Ale to create a hazy, lazy cocktail – perked up with a sharp orange twist.

»

- 50ml (2fl oz) Jim Beam Bourbon
- Fever-Tree Smoky Ginger Ale, to top up
- Twist of orange peel, to garnish

Pour the bourbon into a highball glass filled with ice cubes. Top up with the ginger ale. Garnish with a twist of orange peel.

WITH A TWIST

- 50ml (2fl oz) Jim Beam Bourbon
- 25ml (5 teaspoons) peach purée
- Fever-Tree Smoky Ginger Ale, to top up
- Twist of orange peel, to garnish

Add the bourbon and the peach purée to a highball glass. Top with ice cubes and stir well. Top up with the ginger ale. Garnish with a twist of orange peel.

>>> A little peach liqueur or 1 teaspoon of peach jam would also add a sweet note if you don't have any peach purée.

IRISH HIGHBALL

This classic drink is bubbling with heritage and history. Ireland is home to a proud whiskey-making tradition and thought to be the birthplace of ginger ale. We've brought both together in this simple and yet elegant highball, with a twist of lemon adding a bitter edge to the warmth and spice of the ginger.

«

- 50ml (2fl oz) Jameson Whiskey
- Fever-Tree Ginger Ale, to top up
- Twist of lemon peel, to garnish

Pour the whiskey into a highball glass filled with ice cubes. Top up with the ginger ale. Garnish with a twist of lemon peel.

WITH A TWIST

- 50ml (2fl oz) Jameson Whiskey
- 50ml (2fl oz) apple juice
- Fever-Tree Ginger Ale, to top up
- Twist of lemon peel, to garnish

Pour the whiskey and apple juice into a highball glass filled with ice cubes. Top up with the ginger ale. Garnish with a twist of lemon peel.

SCOTCH HIGHBALL

It's almost impossible to improve a spirit that has the heritage and international recognition of Johnnie Walker's iconic Black Label, but we're giving it a shot with this simple but delicious highball. The cinnamon and clementine notes of Fever-Tree Spiced Orange Ginger Ale blend beautifully with the Black Label, creating an aromatic showcase for the world-famous whisky.

>>

- 50ml (2fl oz) Johnnie Walker Black Label
- Fever-Tree Spiced Orange Ginger Ale, to top up
- Twist of orange peel, to garnish

Pour the whisky into a highball or rocks glass filled with ice cubes. Top up with the ginger ale. Garnish with a twist of orange peel.

WITH A TWIST

- 35ml (2 generous tablespoons) Johnnie Walker Black Label
- 25ml (5 teaspoons) Pedro Ximénez Sherry
- Fever-Tree Spiced Orange Ginger Ale, to top up
- Twist of orange peel, to garnish

Pour the whisky and sherry into a highball glass filled with ice cubes. Top up with the ginger ale. Garnish with a twist of orange peel.

>>> Did you know that sherry casks are an important part of maturing Scotch? So it makes complete sense that a drop of sherry is the perfect addition here.

NEW WORLD HIGHBALL

Australia may not be famous for its whisky yet, but the Starward Distillery has been blazing a tastebud-tingling trail through the spirits industry in recent years. This recipe shows off the fruit-forward flavours of the Victoria-made whisky, adding only subtle hints of lemon and thyme and the gentle bitterness of quinine.

«

- 50ml (2fl oz) Starward Whisky
- Fever-Tree Premium Indian Tonic Water, to top up
- Twist of lemon peel, to garnish
- Thyme sprig, to garnish

Pour the whisky into a highball or rocks glass filled with ice cubes. Top up with the tonic water. Garnish with a twist of lemon peel and a thyme sprig.

WITH A TWIST

- 35ml (2 generous tablespoons) Starward Whisky
- 3 teaspoons dry sherry
- Fever-Tree Premium Indian Tonic Water, to top up
- Twist of lemon peel, to garnish
- Thyme sprig, to garnish

Pour the whisky and sherry into a highball glass filled with ice cubes. Top up with the tonic water. Garnish with a twist of lemon peel and a thyme sprig.

SMOKY COLA HIGHBALL

Created by Dave Broom – whisky aficionado – this drink is a smoky heaven. Using our Distillers Cola, made with Caribbean kola nuts, cold-pressed Mexican limes and high-quality spices including the finest Madagascan vanilla, it is the mixer that will change your mind. Don't knock it until you've tried it!

«

- 50ml (2fl oz) Lagavulin Whisky
- Fever-Tree Distillers Cola, to top up
- Twist of lemon peel, to garnish

Fill a highball glass with ice cubes. Pour over the whisky. Top up with the cola. Garnish with a twist of lemon peel.

WITH A TWIST

- 50ml (2fl oz) Lagavulin Whisky
- 2 teaspoons Pedro Ximénez Sherry
- Fever-Tree Distillers Cola, to top up
- Twist of lemon peel, to garnish

Fill a highball glass with ice cubes. Pour over the whisky and sherry. Top up with the cola. Garnish with a twist of lemon peel.

COGNAC HIGHBALL

At its rich, spirited heart, brandy is still wine – bursting with fresh flavours and deep, earthy aromas. Paired here with sweet vermouth, Fever-Tree Spiced Orange Ginger Ale and a dark berry garnish, the spirit's suppressed flavours are unlocked, enhanced and come bubbling to the fore at full, fruity strength.

»

- 40ml (1¼fl oz) premium Cognac (we like Hennessy)
- 2 teaspoons sweet vermouth
- Fever-Tree Spiced Orange Ginger Ale, to top up
- Blackberry, to garnish
- Blueberry, to garnish

Pour the cognac and sweet vermouth into a highball glass filled with ice cubes. Top up with the ginger ale. Garnish with a blackberry and a blueberry.

WITH A TWIST

- 40ml (1¼fl oz) premium cognac
- 2 teaspoons sweet vermouth
- 3 blackberries, plus an extra blackberry to garnish
- 5 blueberries, plus an extra blueberry to garnish
- Fever-Tree Spiced Orange Ginger Ale, to top up

Pour the Cognac and sweet vermouth into an empty cocktail shaker. Add the blackberries and blueberries. Fill the shaker with ice cubes and shake. Pour the contents of the shaker into a highball glass. Top up with the ginger ale. Garnish with a blackberry and a blueberry.

CUBA LIBRE

This is a fun, flag-waving cocktail that fizzes with spice and simple sweetness. The best of Cuba's rums are alive with flavours of caramel, light cream and soft fruits. We add tangy limes and tasty Fever-Tree Distillers Cola to bring out the best, most exuberant side of the spirit in this iconic drink.

»

- 50ml (2fl oz) premium dark rum (we like Bacardí Anejo Cuatro 4 Year Old Rum)
- Fever-Tree Distillers Cola, to top up
- 2 lime wedges

Fill a highball glass with ice cubes. Pour over the rum. Top up with the cola. Squeeze over the lime wedges, then drop them into the glass as a garnish.

WITH A TWIST

- 50ml (2fl oz) premium dark rum
- 2 teaspoons Kahlúa
- 1 teaspoon fresh lime juice, plus 2 lime wedges to garnish
- Fever-Tree Distillers Cola, to top up

Pour the rum, Kahlúa and lime juice into an empty cocktail shaker. Top up with a good scoop of ice cubes. Shake vigorously for 15 seconds. Pour into a highball glass and add a couple more ice cubes to fill the glass. Top up with the cola. Garnish with the lime wedges.

CHARTREUSE ODDBALL

Here we have a highball for the more adventurous drinker. Chartreuse is a curiously little-known liqueur and its closely guarded recipe contains over 130 secret, spicy botanicals. But it blends beautifully with the gentle bitterness of the tonic water, releasing flavours of herbs and woods into this elegant, unfussy cocktail.

- 50ml (2fl oz) green Chartreuse
- Fever-Tree Premium Indian Tonic Water, to top up
- Lime wedge, to garnish

Pour the Chartreuse into a highball glass filled with ice cubes. Top up with the tonic water. Garnish with a lime wedge.

« WITH A TWIST

- 20ml (4 teaspoons) green Chartreuse
- 20ml (4 teaspoons) maraschino liqueur
- 2 limes, cut into wedges
- Fever-Tree Premium Indian Tonic Water, to top up
- Small rosemary sprig, to garnish
- Green apple slice, to garnish

Pour the Chartreuse and the maraschino liqueur into an empty cocktail shaker. Squeeze over the lime wedges, then discard the shells. Add plenty of ice cubes. Shake for 15 seconds. Pour the contents of the shaker into a highball glass. Top up with the tonic water. Garnish with a rosemary sprig and a green apple slice.

PISCOLA

Popular in South America, pisco is a light, bright grape brandy bursting with aromas of rose and lemon zest. But it's not as delicate as it may sound. In this cocktail, the spirit holds its own admirably against spicy Fever-Tree Distillers Cola and the sharp tang of both lime and grapefruit – with fierce yet floral results.

»

- 50ml (2fl oz) La Diablada Pisco
- Fever-Tree Distillers Cola, to top up
- Lime wedge, to garnish

Pour the pisco into a highball glass filled with ice cubes. Top up with the cola. Garnish with a lime wedge.

WITH A TWIST

- 40ml (1¼fl oz) La Diablada Pisco
- 2 teaspoons peach liqueur
- Fever-Tree Distillers Cola, to top up
- Grapefruit wedge, to garnish

Pour the pisco into a highball glass filled with ice cubes. Add the peach liqueur. Top up with the cola. Garnish with a grapefruit wedge.

COFFEE TONIC

It may sound odd, but coffee aficionados swear by this caffeinated cocktail to get them through warmer weather. Balancing out a bitter shot of espresso, the spiced rum adds sweetness to the drink – before the lemon and thyme flavours of Fever-Tree Mediterranean Tonic Water bring things full circle, for a sharply sour, incredibly refreshing finish. And the non-alcoholic version is almost as good.

«

- 40ml (1¼fl oz) freshly brewed coffee, preferably espresso strength
- Fever-Tree Mediterranean Tonic Water, to top up
- Twist of orange peel, to garnish

Fill a highball glass with ice cubes. Add the shot of espresso. Top up with the tonic water. Holding an orange over the glass to catch the zesty oils, peel off a long twist of orange peel and let it fall into the glass to garnish.

WITH A TWIST

- 50ml (2fl oz) spiced rum
- Fever-Tree Mediterranean Tonic Water, to top up
- 50ml (2fl oz) freshly brewed coffee, preferably espresso strength
- Twist of orange peel, to garnish

Fill a highball glass with ice cubes. Pour over the spiced rum. Top up with the tonic water. Carefully spoon on the freshly brewed coffee so that it floats on top. Holding an orange over the glass to catch the zesty oils, peel off a long twist of orange peel and let it fall into the glass to garnish.

NO & LOW ALCOHOL

5

NO &
LOW ALCOHOL

'What do you drink when you're not drinking alcohol?' Until recently,
the answer to that question might have left you feeling distinctly flat
– a dreary roundabout of saccharine juices, uninspiring cordials and
alcohol-free lagers, dug out unceremoniously from the back of the
cupboard at short notice. There was nothing with the refinement or
delicacy of a classic cocktail, nor the mouthfeel and distinction of a
decent mixed drink. But a quiet revolution has been underway in
recent years, as more and more of us look to cut back on our units –
and today, the non-drinker's cup overflows. The No-Groni Highball, for
example, adds a dazzling new chapter to the long history of its ruby
red forefather.

Classic recipes like our Refreshingly Light Indian Tonic Water with an
aromatic dash of Angostura Bitters, and delicious, fruity perennials like
the St Clement's – good-quality orange juice mixed with equal parts of
our Lemon Tonic – are making their way back into the non-drinker's
repertoire. In addition, there are lower-alcohol takes on established
favoures — the Sherry & Tonic, for example, is a sophisticated long
drink that refreshes and intrigues: a happy middle ground, without any
of the compromise.

BITTERS & TONIC

Sometimes the simplest drinks are the best. Here, the clove and cinnamon flavours of Angostura Bitters are strong enough to substitute for any spirit. Topped up with tonic water and finished with a squeeze of fresh, zesty lemon, this becomes one of the finest – and also most straightforward – low-alcohol cocktails you can mix.

»

- 5 dashes Angostura Bitters
- Fever-Tree Refreshingly Light Indian Tonic Water, to top up
- Lemon wedge, to garnish

Add the bitters to a copa glass filled with ice cubes. Top up with the tonic water. Garnish with a lemon wedge.

WITH A TWIST

- 50ml (2fl oz) freshly squeezed orange juice
- 3 dashes Angostura Bitters
- 2 lemon wedges, plus an extra wedge to garnish
- Fever-Tree Refreshingly Light Indian Tonic Water, to top up

Add the orange juice and bitters to a copa glass filled with ice cubes, then squeeze over the lemon wedges and discard the shells. Top up with the tonic water and garnish with an extra lemon wedge.

NO-GRONI HIGHBALL

This lighter, longer spin on a classic Negroni may be alcohol-free, but it retains all the feisty flavours of the original. Æcorn's impressive aperitifs and Seedlip Spice 94 are simply bursting with botanicals. This herby base blends with the bitterness of Fever-Tree Italian Blood Orange Soda to create an authentic take on the famous cocktail.

- 50ml (2fl oz) Æcorn Bitter
- Fever-Tree Italian Blood Orange Soda
- Orange wedge, to garnish

Pour the Æcorn Bitter into a highball glass filled with ice cubes. Top up with the soda. Garnish with an orange wedge.

« WITH A TWIST

- 25ml (5 teaspoons) Æcorn Bitter
- 25ml (5 teaspoons) Æcorn Aromatic
- 25ml (5 teaspoons) Seedlip Spice 94
- Fever-Tree Italian Blood Orange Soda, to top up
- Blood orange wedge, to garnish

Pour the Æcorn Bitter into a highball glass filled with ice cubes. Add the Æcorn Aromatic and the Seedlip Spice 94. Stir until ice cold, then top with a couple more ice cubes. Top up with the soda. Garnish with a blood orange wedge.

CLASSIC SEEDLIP TONIC

The sharp, tart taste of Seedlip Grove 42 pairs perfectly with a long, iced serving of simple tonic water. The bitterness of the quinine complements the mandarin and lemongrass notes of the non-alcoholic spirit – and the large orange wedge to garnish really drives the citrus flavour home.

>>

- 50ml (2fl oz) Seedlip Grove 42
- Fever-Tree Premium Indian Tonic Water, to top up
- Long twist of orange peel, to garnish

Fill a copa glass with ice cubes. Pour over the Seedlip Grove 42. Top up with the tonic water. Twist the orange peel over the glass, to release the oils, before dropping it into the drink.

WITH A TWIST

- 50ml (2fl oz) Seedlip Grove 42
- 1 teaspoon orange marmalade
- 2 teaspoons Æcorn Bitter
- 200ml (7fl oz) Fever-Tree Premium Indian Tonic Water
- Twist of grapefruit peel, to garnish

Add the Seedlip, orange marmalade and Æcorn Bitter to an empty cocktail shaker. Add a good scoop of ice cubes. Shake vigorously for 10 seconds. Pour into a copa glass and add a couple more ice cubes. Top up with the tonic water. Garnish with a twist of grapefruit peel.

ST CLEMENT'S

'Oranges and Lemons, say the bells of St Clement's'... It's a much-loved nursery rhyme going back at least 300 years, and the St Clement Danes Church in London continues to ring out the famous tune three times a day. The rhyme comes from the shortcut taken through the church's graveyard from the nearby wharf where the fruit was unloaded to the market and sold. Here, our 'lemons' in the form of Lemon Tonic combine perfectly with the orange juice to create the ideal cooling drink for a hot summer's day.

«

- 100ml (3½fl oz) good-quality orange juice
- 100ml (3½fl oz) Fever-Tree Lemon Tonic Water
- Orange wheel, to garnish
- Lemon wheel, to garnish

Fill a highball glass with ice cubes. Pour over the orange juice and the tonic. Garnish with an orange and a lemon wheel.

WITH A TWIST

- 50ml (2fl oz) Aperol or Campari
- 100ml (3½fl oz) Fever-Tree Italian Blood Orange Soda
- 100ml (3½fl oz) Fever-Tree Lemon Tonic Water
- Orange wedge, to garnish
- Lemon wedge, to garnish

Fill a highball glass with ice cubes. Pour over the Aperol or Campari. Add the soda and tonic. Garnish with an orange and a lemon wedge.

>>> For an even more flavoursome drink, squeeze some additonal fresh orange wedges into the glass.

GUNNER

Another cooling classic, this drink is a Hong Kong original, where it has been enjoyed for decades to help soothe the effects of the city's soaring humidity. At the world-renowned Captain's Bar in the Mandarin Oriental it is especially cooling, served in traditional chilled silver tankards. If you are lucky enough to become a regular, your name can be inscribed on to one of the hallowed vessels.

«

- 3 dashes Angostura Bitters
- 200ml (7fl oz) Fever-Tree Ginger Ale
- Fever-Tree Ginger Beer, to top up
- 1 lime wedge

Fill a highball glass with ice cubes. Add the bitters. Pour over the ginger ale and top up with the ginger beer. Squeeze in the lime wedge and drop into the glass as a garnish.

WITH A TWIST

- 50ml (2fl oz) sweet red vermouth
- 3 dashes Angostura Bitters
- 200ml (7fl oz) Fever-Tree Ginger Ale
- Fever-Tree Ginger Beer, to top up
- 2 lime wedges

Fill a highball glass with ice cubes. Add the vermouth and bitters. Pour over the ginger ale and top up with the ginger beer. Squeeze in the lime wedges and drop into the glass as a garnish.

>>> For a higher-ABV drink, a premium dark rum would work wonderfully too.

SICILIAN SHANDY

The shandy is a much-loved way to temper the strength of your lager or beer and is a wonderfully refreshing drink. The name comes from the old London term 'shandygaff', which was slang for beer mixed with lemonade or ginger beer. Over the years, we have lost the 'gaff' and lemonade has become the go-to mixer for shandy. Here, Sicily's finest lemons complement your favourite lager perfectly, although if you do prefer a darker ale, you can try it with our gorgeous ginger beer too.

- 250ml (8½fl oz) Fever-Tree Sicilian Lemonade
- Premium lager or beer, to top up

Half fill a beer glass with the Sicilian lemonade. Top up carefully with lager or beer so that the foam doesn't spill over the top.

WITH A TWIST »

- A pinch of good-quality salt
- 250ml (8½fl oz) Fever-Tree Sicilian Lemonade
- Premium lager, to top up
- 3 lime wedges

Add the salt and lemonade to a beer glass. Top up carefully with the lager so that the foam doesn't spill over the top. Squeeze the lime wedges into the drink then drop them into the glass to garnish.

LYRE'S APERITIF

When you're steering clear of alcohol, you don't have to sacrifice strong flavours as well. With Lyre's aromatic Apéritif Dry and the double herby hit of thyme and Fever-Tree Mediterranean Tonic Water, this highball is as dry as it is delicious.

- 50ml (2fl oz) Lyre's Apéritif Dry
- 3 lemon wedges
- Fever-Tree Mediterranean Tonic Water, to top up
- Thyme sprig, to garnish

Pour the Lyre's Apéritif Dry into a highball glass filled with ice cubes. Squeeze over and then drop in the lemon wedges. Top up with the tonic water. Garnish with a thyme sprig.

« WITH A TWIST

- 50ml (2fl oz) Lyre's Apéritif Dry
- 1 thyme sprig, plus an extra sprig to garnish
- 2 teaspoons sugar syrup (see page 15)
- 3 lemon wedges, plus an extra wedge to garnish
- Fever-Tree Mediterranean Tonic Water, to top up

Add the Lyre's Apéritif Dry to an empty cocktail shaker with the thyme sprig and sugar syrup. Squeeze over and then drop in the lemon wedges. Top up with ice cubes. Shake hard for 15 seconds, then pour the contents of the shaker into a highball glass. Top up with the tonic water. Garnish with a lemon wedge and a thyme sprig.

WHITE GRAPE & APRICOT

Grapes lead the way in this fruity, refreshing, sparkling cocktail.
The white grape and apricot flavours of the soda send a dynamic,
tongue-tingling fizz through the tart fruits used as a garnish.

»

- 50ml (2fl oz) Lillet Blanc
- Fever-Tree White Grape & Apricot Soda, to top up
- White grape, to garnish
- Twist of lemon peel, to garnish

Fill a large wine glass with ice cubes. Pour over the Lillet. Top up with
the soda. Garnish with a white grape and a twist of lemon peel.

WITH A TWIST

- 1 orange wedge
- 1 lemon wedge, plus a twist of lemon peel, to garnish
- 25ml (5 teaspoons) Lillet Blanc
- 25ml (5 teaspoons) Campari
- Fever-Tree White Grape & Apricot Soda, to top up
- White grape, to garnish

Fill a tall glass with ice cubes. Squeeze over the orange and lemon wedge, then drop
them into the glass. Pour over the Lillet and Campari. Top up with the soda. Garnish
with a white grape and a twist of lemon peel.

SHERRY & TONIC

Sherry is one of the world's most versatile wines. From dry to sweet, it crops up in cocktails from the Bamboo to the Bloody Mary. In this drink, the Spanish wine is mixed simply with Fever-Tree Mediterranean Tonic Water, whose subtle herby flavours and saline qualities are given an opportunity to fizz to the fore.

«

- 60ml (4 tablespoons) dry sherry
- Fever-Tree Mediterranean Tonic Water, to top up
- Lemon wedge, to garnish

Pour the sherry into a highball glass filled with ice cubes. Top up with the tonic water. Garnish with a lemon wedge.

WITH A TWIST

- 60ml (4 tablespoons) Pedro Ximénez Sherry
- Fever-Tree Spiced Orange Ginger Ale, to top up
- Orange wedge, to garnish

Pour the sherry into a highball glass filled with ice cubes. Top up with the ginger ale. Garnish with an orange wedge.

APEROL BLOOD ORANGE SPRITZ

You can never have too much orange in an Aperol Spritz. That's why, instead of regular soda water, this spin on the classic aperitif adds Fever-Tree Italian Blood Orange Soda, as well as Cointreau and a thick orange wedge, to make each sip as juicy as possible.

»

- 50ml (2fl oz) Aperol
- Fever-Tree Italian Blood Orange Soda, to top up
- Thick orange wedge, to garnish

Pour the Aperol into a copa or wine glass filled with ice cubes. Top up with the soda. Garnish with a thick orange wedge.

WITH A TWIST

- 35ml (2 generous tablespoons) Aperol
- 3 teaspoons Cointreau
- A splash of prosecco
- Fever-Tree Italian Blood Orange Soda, to top up
- Thick orange wedge, to garnish
- Mint leaf, to garnish

Pour the Aperol and Cointreau into a copa or wine glass filled with ice cubes. Add a splash of prosecco. Top up with the soda. Garnish with a thick orange wedge and a mint leaf.

PITCHER
PERFECT

PITCHER PERFECT

The great irony of mixing the perfect drink when you're entertaining is that you often never get to enjoy it yourself. At parties from Preston to Perugia, it happens like clockwork – as soon as the finishing touches have been added to that exquisitely proportioned refreshment (a twist of perfumed orange peel here, a careful dash of bitters there), an acquaintance will emerge over your right shoulder with a familiar refrain: 'That looks nice. Mind making me one?' Before you know it, you've strapped on an apron and stationed yourself behind the bar for the night – while your own dear, sweet little Campari Spritz withers and melts on the mantelpiece, and the party whirs on without you.

Never fear! Put down the cocktail shaker! Wipe off your brow! In this chapter, we've prepared a set of simple pitcher recipes to share around at your next party or picnic so that you can spend less time making drinks and more time drinking and socializing. You'll find established classics – such as the Pimm's Pitcher or the Sicilian Iced Tea – as well as some low- and no-alcohol alternatives. And, of course, a few long, delicous G&T twists.

All the recipes here use a 2-litre (2-quart) jug, three-quarters filled with ice cubes, which will give you approximately 1 litre (1 quart) of drink to share around. If you use large glasses, as pictured throughout this chapter, you'll serve around four people per pitcher, while smaller glasses will stretch the drink quantity further. If you want to make more, it's a good idea, in advance of the event, to add ice cubes to the jug you want to use and measure how much liquid it holds and adjust your chosen recipe accordingly.

APPLE, GIN & GINGER PITCHER

This is the perfect pitcher for a picnic. The light, fresh flavour combination of crisp apple and spicy ginger is tried and tested, and Tanqueray's London Dry Gin blends beautifully into the mix. Add bright mint and sharp lemon, and you won't find a better sun-soaked, sparkling drink anywhere.

Makes 4 large drinks in a 2-litre (2-quart) pitcher

- 200ml (7fl oz) Tanqueray London Dry Gin
- 2 lemons, cut into quarters
- 150ml (5fl oz) good-quality apple juice
- 650ml (22fl oz) Fever-Tree Ginger Ale
- Mint sprig, to garnish
- Apple wedges, to garnish

Fill a pitcher three-quarters full with ice cubes. Pour over the gin. Squeeze over the lemon quarters, then drop them into the pitcher. Add the apple juice and top up with the ginger ale. Garnish with a mint sprig and apple wedges.

>>> If you have a little time, mix up the drink without the ice or ginger ale. Add the mint sprig and apple wedges and let them soak for 1 hour, to add even more flavour. Just before serving, add ice cubes and top up with the ginger ale.

STRAWBERRY & ELDERFLOWER COLLINS

Strawberries add a sharp sweetness to this classic gin cocktail. They also give it a beautiful blush of colour. When the bright, leafy mint and flowery essence of elderflower chime in, you're treated to a long, refreshing drink with all the aromas, tones and textures of an English country garden.

Makes 4 large drinks in a 2-litre (2-quart) pitcher

- 4 strawberries, halved, plus a few extra halves to garnish
- 200ml (7fl oz) Hendrick's Gin
- 2 lemons, cut into quarters
- 800ml (27fl oz) Fever-Tree Elderflower Tonic Water
- Mint sprigs, to garnish

Add the strawberries to an empty pitcher. Pour in the gin. Squeeze over the lemon quarters, then drop them into the pitcher. Stir well and leave for 10 minutes. Fill the pitcher three-quarters full with ice cubes. Top up with the tonic water. Serve with a mint sprig and a strawberry half in each glass to garnish.

>>> If you don't have any fresh strawberries, or you're in a bit of a hurry, you could add a fruit-flavoured liqueur instead to give flavour and colour to this cocktail. Add 50ml (2fl oz) of your favourite liqueur and reduce the gin quantity to 150ml (5fl oz).

RASPBERRY VODKA & LIME SODA

Few drinks can't be improved by the addition of a couple of ripe, juicy raspberries – and the classic Vodka & Lime Soda is no exception. We've paired the citrus-forward notes of crisp Grey Goose Vodka with Fever-Tree Mexican Lime Soda, before adding sweet raspberries and rich Chambord for a delicious, decadent pitcher.

Makes 4 large drinks in a 2-litre (2-quart) pitcher

- 200ml (7fl oz) Grey Goose Vodka
- 50ml (2fl oz) Chambord
- 1 lemon, cut into quarters
- 800ml (27fl oz) Fever-Tree Mexican Lime Soda
- Raspberries, to garnish

Fill a pitcher three-quarters full with ice cubes. Pour over the vodka and the Chambord. Squeeze over the lemon quarters, then drop them into the pitcher. Top up with the soda. Garnish with raspberries.

>>> If you don't have any Chambord, soak a handful of raspberries in the vodka for a few hours before making the cocktail. This extracts their natural flavour and colour, and heightens the taste of the drink.

WATERMELON & GINGER SUMMER COOLER

Do try to find the time to soak the watermelon in the vodka before you serve it up – it will elevate this super-refreshing cocktail to a different level. But even if you don't, with the clean taste of Ketel One Vodka, the fruity kick of Cointreau or Grand Marnier and the warming fizz of Fever-Tree Ginger Ale, this is a greatest-hits pitcher full of fantastic flavours.

Makes 4 large drinks in a 2-litre (2-quart) pitcher

- 150ml (5fl oz) Ketel One Vodka
- 50ml (2fl oz) Cointreau or Grand Marnier
- ½ watermelon (deseeded)
- 2 limes, cut into quarters
- 800ml (27fl oz) Fever-Tree Ginger Ale
- Mint sprigs, to garnish

Fill a pitcher three-quarters full with ice cubes. Pour over the vodka and Cointreau or Grand Marnier. Cut a few cubes of the watermelon and set aside for a garnish. Chop the rest into wedges and add these to the pitcher. Squeeze over the lime quarters, then drop them into the pitcher. Top up with the ginger ale. Garnish with the watermelon cubes and mint sprigs.

>>> If you have time, leave the watermelon cubes soaking in the spirits for 1 hour before preparing the rest of the cocktail and serving. This will add more colour and flavour to your final drink.

WHITE WINE SPRITZER

This spritzer swaps out spirits in favour of Sauvignon Blanc –
and it does so to great effect. With wine, the flavours of the juicy
orange and the rosemary are given space to shine, and the Fever-
Tree Mediterranean Tonic Water can offer up its savoury sparkle
without the risk of being overpowered.

Makes 4 large drinks in a 2-litre (2-quart) pitcher

- 500ml (17fl oz) Sauvignon Blanc or your favourite white wine
- 1 orange, sliced into wheels
- 500ml (17fl oz) Fever-Tree Mediterranean Tonic Water
- Small rosemary sprigs, to garnish

Fill a pitcher three-quarters full with ice cubes. Pour in the white wine.
Add the orange wheels. Top up with the tonic water. To serve, pour into
wine glasses filled with ice cubes and garnish each one with a small
rosemary sprig.

>>> You can replace 100ml (3½fl oz) of the white wine with the same amount of dry white vermouth
to add more depth, subtle sweetness and some floral tones. And adding a couple of herb sprigs,
such as rosemary or thyme, to the pitcher will give a drier, herbier finish.

SANGRIA

Sangria may mean 'bloodletting' in Spanish, but don't let that put you off this flavourful, refreshing drink. Our rich take on the traditional cocktail mixes vibrant Rioja with bold brandy, before topping up with sharp, sparkling Fever-Tree Italian Blood Orange Soda and adding a fruity garnish to create a cocktail with a lingering, lemony finish.

Makes 4 large drinks in a 2-litre (2-quart) pitcher

- 1 orange, cut into 6–8 wedges
- 1 lemon, cut into 6–8 wedges
- 400ml (14fl oz) Spanish Rioja or your favourite red wine
- 100ml (3½fl oz) premium brandy
- 500ml (17fl oz) Fever-Tree Italian Blood Orange Soda
- Mint sprigs, to garnish

Fill a pitcher three-quarters full with ice cubes. Squeeze over the orange and lemon wedges, then drop them into the pitcher. Pour over the red wine and the brandy. Top up with the soda. To serve, pour into wine glasses filled with ice cubes, adding some of the citrus wedges from the pitcher into each one, and a mint sprig to garnish.

>>> If you have time, mix together the fruit, wine and brandy and let it infuse for 1 hour before adding the ice and soda, for a more intense fruity flavour. And you can swap the red wine for a sparkling rosé and add pomegranate seeds for an autumnal take on a classic sangria.

PALOMA PITCHER

The Margarita may be Mexico's most famous cocktail, but the Paloma is the nation's fruity favourite. This pitcher is the perfect way to give it a try, mixing the peppery zest of Patrón Silver Tequila with salt, limes and a balanced burst of Fever-Tree Sparkling Pink Grapefruit or Lemon Tonic Water.

Makes 4 large drinks in a 2-litre (2-quart) pitcher

- 200ml (7fl oz) Patrón Silver Tequila
- 2 limes, cut into quarters
- A pinch of salt
- 800ml (27fl oz) Fever-Tree Sparkling Pink Grapefruit or Lemon Tonic Water

Fill a pitcher three-quarters full with ice cubes. Pour over the tequila. Squeeze over the lime quarters, then drop them into the pitcher. Add a pinch of salt. Top up with the sparkling pink grapefruit or tonic water.

>>> To increase the depth of flavour, you could add 20ml (4 teaspoons) agave syrup. Pour the tequila into the empty pitcher, then add the agave syrup. Stir gently until the syrup dissolves before topping up with ice cubes, preparing the rest of the cocktail and serving.

NEGRONI PITCHER

The Negroni is itself a twist on an existing cocktail, created when an Italian count asked his bartender to swap the soda water in his Americano for gin. This Sipsmith-fuelled spin on the now-classic Negroni carries on the tradition of tweaking, adding Fever-Tree Italian Blood Orange Soda for a longer, more refreshing finish.

Makes 4 large drinks in a 2-litre (2-quart) pitcher

- 100ml (3½fl oz) Sipsmith London Dry Gin
- 100ml (3½fl oz) Campari
- 100ml (3½fl oz) Martini Rosso Vermouth
- 700ml (23½fl oz) Fever-Tree Italian Blood Orange Soda
- Orange wedges, to garnish

Fill a pitcher three-quarters full with ice cubes. Pour in the gin, Campari and vermouth. Top up with the soda. To serve, pour into rocks glasses filled with ice cubes and garnish each one with an orange wedge.

> > > For a sweeter-style drink, you can replace the gin with premium bourbon.

MEZCAL MULE

This Mule has a kick! Combining the earthy spice of Fever-Tree Ginger Beer with the deep, smoky depths of Del Maguey Mezcal, this is a cocktail that unleashes the full fruity, nutty flavour of the Mexican spirit. We've finished it off with fresh, sharp lime to create a party in a pitcher.

Makes 4 large drinks in a 2-litre (2-quart) pitcher

- 200ml (7fl oz) Del Maguey Mezcal
- 2 limes, halved, plus extra lime wedges, to garnish
- 800ml (27fl oz) Fever-Tree Ginger Beer

Fill a pitcher three-quarters full with ice cubes. Pour over the mezcal. Squeeze over the lime halves, then discard the shells. Top up with the ginger beer. To serve, pour into rocks glasses filled with ice cubes and garnish each one with a lime wedge.

> > > Add a few red chilli slices to the pitcher for an even mightier kick to this Mule.

DARK & STORMY PITCHER

The Dark & Stormy has its origins in 19th-century Bermuda and was created when the British Royal Navy docked at Ireland Island and officers began brewing their own ginger beer. The sailors soon mixed it with their rations of rum to create a cocktail – using the same Gosling's Black Seal Rum that we still recommend today.

Makes 4 large drinks in a 2-litre (2-quart) pitcher

- 200ml (7fl oz) Gosling's Black Seal Rum
- 2 limes, cut into wedges, plus extra wedges to garnish
- 800ml (27fl oz) Fever-Tree Ginger Beer

Fill a pitcher three-quarters full with ice cubes. Pour over the rum. Squeeze over the lime wedges, then drop them into the pitcher. Top up with the ginger beer. To serve, pour into highball glasses filled with ice cubes and garnish each one with a lime wedge.

RASPBERRY MULE

This is the perfect drink for a pitcher. Fresh raspberries are supercharged by Chambord's rich berry liqueur. Spicy ginger beer fizzes through, with a bitter hit of lime to finish. And with Belvedere's extraordinarily pure vodka at its heart, this is a super-sized sparkling treat.

Makes 4 large drinks in a 2-litre (2-quart) pitcher

- 150ml (5fl oz) Belvedere Vodka
- 50ml (2fl oz) Chambord or other raspberry liqueur
- 2 limes, cut into quarters
- 800ml (27fl oz) Fever-Tree Ginger Beer
- Raspberries, to garnish
- Mint sprigs, to garnish

Fill a pitcher three-quarters full with ice cubes. Pour over the vodka and Chambord or other raspberry liqueur. Squeeze over the lime quarters, then drop them into the pitcher. Top up with the ginger beer. To serve, pour into rocks glasses filled with ice cubes and garnish each one with a raspberry and a mint sprig.

>>> For added flair, dust a little icing sugar over the top of the garnishes in each glass.

PIMM'S PITCHER

Nothing says summer quite like a pitcher full of Pimm's. The recipe itself is legendary – strawberries, orange, mint and cucumber mixed with the herby, fruity notes of the world-famous Pimm's No. 1 Cup. In our version, we've added Fever-Tree Cucumber Tonic Water for an extra fizz of salad-sweet freshness.

Makes 4 large drinks in a 2-litre (2-quart) pitcher

- 300ml (10fl oz) Pimm's No. 1 Cup
- 2 oranges, cut into wedges, plus an extra orange, sliced
- 8 strawberries, halved
- ½ cucumber, sliced
- 12 mint leaves, plus extra mint sprigs to garnish
- 700ml (23½fl oz) Fever-Tree Cucumber Tonic Water

Fill a pitcher three-quarters full with ice cubes. Pour over the Pimm's. Squeeze the orange wedges over, then discard the shells. Add the orange slices, strawberry halves and cucumber slices. Tear the mint leaves, then add them to the pitcher. Top up with the tonic water and stir gently. To serve, pour into highball glasses, adding some of the fruit from the pitcher into each one to garnish.

> >>> You could add Champagne to taste to elevate this drink even further. And for a spicier, less sweet version, add small sprigs of rosemary, some raspberries and a handful of pink peppercorns to the pitcher instead of the orange slices, strawberries and cucumber.

GIN CUCUMBER PITCHER

For a crisp, subtly sweet picnic pitcher, there are few better options than this classic cooler. Melon and cucumber are key summer flavours, and they blend beautifully with gin, lemon and Fever-Tree Cucumber Tonic Water. With a wedge of bright pink watermelon to garnish, this becomes a first-class thirst-quencher.

Makes 4 large drinks in a 2-litre (2-quart) pitcher

- 200ml (7fl oz) premium gin, preferably Hendrick's or Aviation
- 1 watermelon, deseeded and cut into large slices
- 25ml (5 teaspoons) sugar syrup (see page 15)
- 800ml (27fl oz) Fever-Tree Cucumber Tonic Water
- 2 lemons, halved

Fill a pitcher three-quarters full with ice cubes. Pour over the gin. Add 12 watermelon slices and the sugar syrup. Top up with the tonic water. Squeeze over the lemon halves, then discard the shells. To serve, pour into highball glasses and garnish each one with a wedge of the remaining watermelon.

APEROL & ITALIAN BLOOD ORANGE PITCHER

When one glass of Aperol doesn't quite scratch that spritz itch, this bright orange pitcher is guaranteed to do the job. Adding good-quality prosecco and bittersweet Fever-Tree Italian Blood Orange Soda, this is a supersized spin on the classic aperitif. And with those orange wheels floating on top, it makes the perfect summer centrepiece.

Makes 4 large drinks in a 2-litre (2-quart) pitcher

- 200ml (7fl oz) Aperol
- 350ml (12fl oz) good-quality prosecco or other white sparkling wine
- 500ml (17fl oz) Fever-Tree Italian Blood Orange Soda
- 1 orange, cut into wheels, plus twists of orange peel to garnish

Fill a pitcher three-quarters full with ice cubes. Pour over the Aperol and the prosecco or other white sparkling wine. Top up with the soda. Add the orange wheels and stir gently. To serve, pour into wine glasses filled with plenty of ice cubes and garnish each one with a twist of orange peel.

SICILIAN ICED TEA

When iced tea first appeared over 150 years ago, it was seen as a novelty. This bourbon-brewed cocktail version has a herby kick of mint and soft sweetness from the peach liqueur, and the Fever-Tree Sicilian Lemonade gives it a delightful, long, refreshing finish.

Makes 4 large drinks in a 2-litre (2-quart) pitcher

- 400ml (14fl oz) boiling water
- 2 English Breakfast tea bags
- 150ml (5fl oz) premium bourbon, preferably Bulleit
- 50ml (2fl oz) peach liqueur
- 15 mint leaves
- 500ml (17fl oz) Fever-Tree Sicilian Lemonade
- Peach slices, to garnish

Pour the measured boiling water over the tea bags in a large mug or pot and brew the tea for 1 minute. Remove the tea bags and wait until the tea is cool, then place in the refrigerator to chill. When the tea is cold, fill a pitcher three-quarters full with ice cubes. Pour over the bourbon, peach liqueur and chilled tea. Add the mint leaves and stir gently. Top up with the lemonade. To serve, pour into highball glasses filled with plenty of ice cubes and garnish each one with a peach slice.

>>> To heighten the intensity of the peach flavour and for a sweeter cocktail, add some peach slices to the tea once it has cooled and leave in the refrigerator for 2 hours to infuse. Add the peach slices to the pitcher along with the chilled tea.

APPLE & GINGER ALE COOLER

This non-alcoholic pitcher is a lovely, simple drink for sharing. Choose a good-quality apple juice (we prefer the cloudy type, for its depth of flavour) and blend it with Fever-Tree Ginger Ale. Mixed over ice, the combination of cool citrus and warm, earthy notes at the heart of this drink serves up a tingling taste sensation.

Makes 4 large drinks in a 2-litre (2-quart) pitcher

- 500ml (17fl oz) good-quality apple juice, preferably cloudy
- 500ml (17fl oz) Fever-Tree Ginger Ale
- 2 limes, each cut into 6 wedges, plus extra lime wheels to garnish
- Red chilli slices, to garnish

Fill a pitcher three-quarters full with ice cubes. Pour over the apple juice. Top up with the ginger ale. Squeeze the lime wedges over, then drop them into the pitcher. Stir gently. To serve, pour into highball glasses and garnish each one with a lime wheel and red chilli slices.

CRANBERRY TONIC

This refreshing pitcher sparkles with sharp, tart flavours.
The sour-sweet cranberries and fresh pink grapefruit work
wonderfully together to complement the bitter herby notes of the
Fever-Tree Mediterranean Tonic Water and the earthy quality of
the mint. Remember, if you slap or tear your mint leaves before
adding them to the glass, the flavour will flourish.

Makes 4 large drinks in a 2-litre (2-quart) pitcher

- 500ml (17fl oz) good-quality cranberry juice,
preferably Ocean Spray
- 5 pink grapefruit wedges, plus a few thin grapefruit
slices to garnish
- 15 mint leaves, plus extra sprigs to garnish
- 500ml (17fl oz) Fever-Tree Mediterranean Tonic Water

Fill a pitcher three-quarters full with ice cubes. Pour over the cranberry
juice. Squeeze over the grapefruit wedges, then drop them into the
pitcher. Slap the mint leaves to release their aromas (see page 12), then
add them to the pitcher. Top up with the tonic water. To serve, pour into
highball glasses and garnish each one with a mint sprig and a thin pink
grapefruit slice.

CUCUMBER COOLER

The salad-sweet flavour of cucumber is a perfect match for the complex flavours of London Dry gin. Throw in the clean, natural flavours of fresh mint and zesty lime juice, and this pitcher becomes the coolest cooler you'll mix all summer.

Makes 4 large drinks in a 2-litre (2-quart) pitcher

- 200ml (7fl oz) premium London Dry gin (we like Bombay Sapphire)
- 15–20 mint leaves
- 3 limes, halved, plus extra lime wheels to garnish
- 800ml (27fl oz) Fever-Tree Cucumber Tonic Water

Fill a pitcher three-quarters full with ice cubes. Pour over the gin. Slap the mint leaves to release their aromas (see page 12), then add them to the pitcher. Squeeze over the lime halves, then discard the shells. Top up with the tonic water. To serve, pour into highball glasses and garnish each one with a lime wheel.

CUCUMBER SPRITZ

In this spritz, the green apple and gooseberry flavours of Sauvignon Blanc mix majestically with the peach and pear notes of delicate St-Germain elderflower liqueur. Fever-Tree Cucumber Tonic Water adds both sparkle and a slightly savoury taste to balance, before mint finishes off the fizz with a refreshing, herby hit.

Makes 4 large drinks in a 2-litre (2-quart) pitcher

- 300ml (10fl oz) white wine, preferably Sauvignon Blanc
- 60ml (4 tablespoons) St-Germain elderflower liqueur
- 600ml (20fl oz) Fever-Tree Cucumber Tonic Water
- 20 mint leaves, plus extra sprigs to garnish
- Cucumber slices to garnish

Fill a pitcher three-quarters full with ice cubes. Pour over the white wine and the elderflower liqueur. Slap the mint leaves to release their aromas (see page 12), then add them to the pitcher and stir gently. Top up with the tonic water. To serve, pour into wine glasses and add a cucumber slice and mint sprig to each to garnish.

RASPBERRY COSMO PITCHER

The Cosmopolitan was created in 1980s New York, and has been balancing sweet and tart flavours in fruity, citrusy style ever since. Its only fault? There's never enough of it! Thankfully, this recipe – with fresh raspberries, cranberry juice, orange liqueur and Fever-Tree Mexican Lime Soda – offers a delicious pitcher-sized solution.

Makes 4 large drinks in a 2-litre (2-quart) pitcher

- 200ml (7fl oz) premium citrus vodka
- 40ml (1¼fl oz) Cointreau or triple sec
- 100ml (3½fl oz) cranberry juice
- 10 raspberries, plus a few extra to garnish
- 650ml (22fl oz) Fever-Tree Mexican Lime Soda

Fill a pitcher three-quarters full with ice cubes. Pour over the vodka and Cointreau or triple sec. Add the cranberry juice and the raspberries. Top up with the soda. To serve, pour into highball glasses filled with ice cubes and garnish each one with a raspberry.

GLOSSARY

UK	US
caster sugar	superfine sugar
cloudy apple juice	apple cider
copa glass	copa de Balon glass; gin balloon glass
cordial	concentrated syrup
crème de mûre	blackberry liqueur
dark chocolate	semisweet chocolate
dried chilli flakes	dried red pepper flakes
icing sugar	confectioner's sugar; powdered sugar
jug	pitcher
lemonade	lemon-flavored soda
Fever-Tree Mexican Lime Soda	Fever-Tree Sparkling Lime & Yuzu
Fever-Tree Premium Soda Water	Fever-Tree Premium Club Soda
rocks glass/tumbler	old-fashioned glass
Fever-Tree Sicilian Lemonade	Fever-Tree Sparkling Lemon
spirits	liquor
top up	top off

INDEX

ACKNOWLEDGEMENTS

Like *The Art of Mixing*, this book couldn't have been brought to life without hard graft and effort from all the team at Fever-Tree HQ – Ollie Winters and Florence Wong were instrumental in co-ordinating and crafting the book, and particular thanks to Craig Harper whose endless knowledge and creative mind for drinks formed the backbone of this collection of recipes. His team, Jaz Arwand, Gavin Bruce and David Barber, were also instrumental in road-testing and writing some of these brilliant recipes. A huge thank you to our co-founder Tim Warrillow for his vision and guidance in pulling the book together.

But of course, *Easy Mixing* wouldn't be published without the brilliant team at Octopus Publishing, especially head publisher Denise Bates, who, once again, has brought her calmness and experience to the project to bring it to fruition. Thank you to Pauline Bache and Joe Bullmore for turning our ramblings into beautiful prose; and Yasia Williams-Leedham, Issy Croker, Emily Ezekiel and Missy Flynn for their expertise in crafting and showing each drink in all its brilliance.